FIND YOUR PASSION AND
LIVE THE DREAM!

# FIND YOUR PASSION AND LIVE THE DREAM!

Gene K. J. Kopczyk

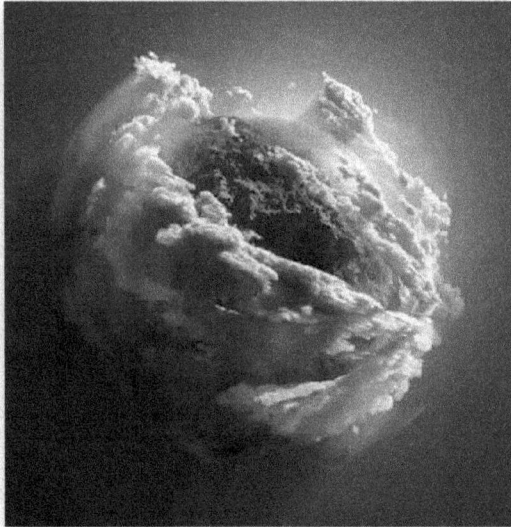

You're a spirit driving a flesh-coated skeleton made from stardust, riding a rock, hurling through space. What do you have to be afraid of?

ISBN: 0692687750
ISBN 13: 9780692687758

# TABLE OF CONTENTS

# DEDICATION

*I would like to take a minute to dedicate this work:*

*To my Lord and Savior, who strengthens me that I may do all things. I love You.*

*To my wife Jennifer (Monkey), thank you for your unending support and belief in me. It has helped me accomplish so much in my life. I hope in some way you understand how much you mean to me. I love you.*

*To my dad for giving me the tools and helping me to understand that "I could do anything if I just got my attitude in check." You were right, Pop! I love you.*

*To my mom for instilling in me that "the sky was not the limit." I love you.*

*To Doug and Vickie, who took me in when times were at a low, as if I were already family. I love you.*

*To all the people who have loved and hated me throughout my life at different times: I would not be the person I am today if you had not done that. I love you for it.*

*And of course to you, the reader, wherever you may be located physically and wherever you are in your life. It's not over until you say it's over. It's not over until you find your passion and live your dream. Dream bigger.*

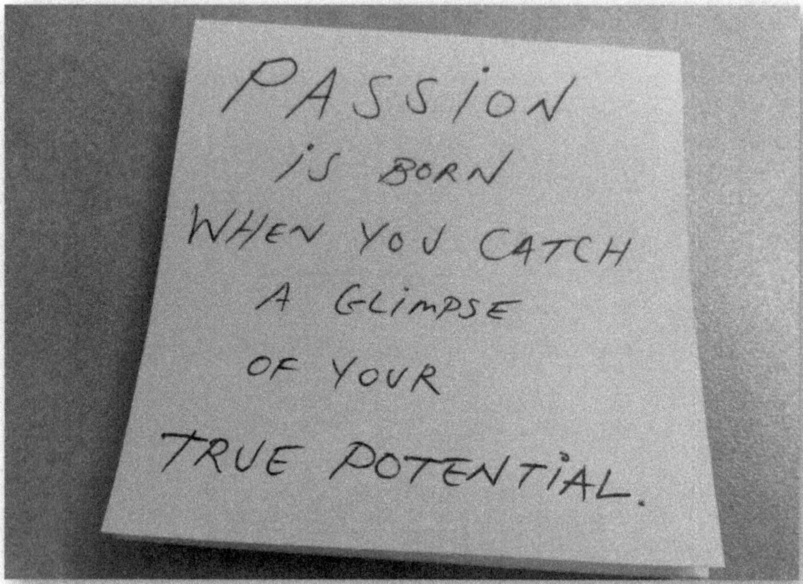
PASSION
IS BORN
WHEN YOU CATCH
A GLIMPSE
OF YOUR
TRUE POTENTIAL.

# PREFACE

HAVE YOU EVER woken up in the morning, looked around, and thought, *How did I get here? This is not the life I wanted. I'm not doing the things I wanted to do. I'm not happy with where this road is taking me. Yet how do I move on from this rut I seem to be stuck in? What's the key to moving forward and feeling fulfilled?* I know I have. I know that I am not the only one who has. While I cannot promise you that you will find every answer to every question on your journey, I can promise you that the book you have picked up—the one you're reading right now—will give you a great starting point.

Please note as you begin reading that I am not going to tell anything that you don't already know. I am not going to teach anything that you have not already heard. My only hope in writing this book is to inspire you to look and think about the world and the opportunities you have in a different light—so that maybe, when you see your opportunity, you won't settle for less because you don't realize what you have in your hands. You know how when you put a stick in the water, and it looks bent? The stick is the opportunities that we have within our reach. But we don't take them because they appear to be misshapen and do not fit with how we expect the opportunity to look. The stick only appears bent because of the way the light refracts to a more horizontal direction as it passes through the water's surface. Because the light hitting the stick above the water is not affected by the refraction, your brain interprets the whole stick as being bent at the point it touches the water. In the same way, your passion and your dreams may not fit the way you think they should. What you find is your brain interpreting them with its best guess at how opportunities and dreams should look. I want you to understand that the stick is really straight; you just have to remove it from the water. Once you accomplish that, your mind will begin to see things in a different light. It will start to show you paths and help you make better decisions to straighten out problems in ways that you could not have previously imagined. Then nothing can stop you!

Isn't it about time? Time for you to step out and become the person you've always wanted to be. Time to become the person you knew you could be. Time for you to start thinking for yourself. Time for you to stop talking yourself out of what you really want to do. Time to believe in yourself again and to know that you can handle anything that comes your way. Time to start ignoring the negative talkers and the armchair warriors. Time to start turning those cant's into cans. Time to stop making excuses. Time to stop letting others steal time from you. Time to see just how much you can stretch yourself and grow. Time to stop waiting for the right moment. Time to take the leap. Time to see just how much the universe has in store for you. Time to find your passion and live the dream!

> "Shoot for the moon. Even if you miss you'll be amongst the stars!" —Les Brown

> "Everything you want is just outside your comfort zone!" —Tony Horton

> "Never explain, never complain. No one gives a damn anyway!" —John Z. DeLorean

There are no limits to
what you can accomplish,

except the limits you place
on your own
THINKING

# INTRODUCTION

My story begins in 1975, when I was born as the youngest child in my family. Because of this, my siblings always felt that my parents gave me an advantage over them because, well, I was the baby. Over time, my elementary school counselor branded me as "learning disabled" after I was diagnosed with ADD (attention deficit disorder) in my childhood. For a long time, I brought home Ds and Fs and was able to hide behind the excuse of the label that was put on me. As I continued onward in my education, my father told me one day, as we were walking out of a parent-teacher conference, that I could do anything if I would just get my attitude in check. I think now that maybe he saw that my poor attitude was more of a facade to hide my insecurities behind. This way no one could see the way I really viewed the world.

I had been given a label, and in order to change my attitude, I would have to change how I thought not only about that label but also about the world in general. So I began to do this a little at a time: my grades improved, I made the dean's list, and I became addicted to the positive attention I could get just by performing at a level slightly better than I had been performing at previously. See, I figured out that most people give up. I heard someone say once, "Do you know what makes someone extraordinary? It's that little 'extra' at the front of the word ordinary." I took that quote to heart and would always do just a little extra.

That inspired me to continue to think about life differently, and before I knew it, I was off to the University of Michigan. While there, I made the university dean's list and got a number of other awards. Also while in college, I met my wife, Jennifer, where we worked together, and that was over twenty-five years ago. I think she always knew I was different, but in a good way. I continued to look for information and admire people who thought differently. While a lot of them were laughed at, they were very successful. As time went on, I decided that I wanted to be my own boss and not have to work for someone. In 2000 I filed for the name of my company, and we have grown ever since.

My wife and I branched out into a successful fitness studio, and we are able to help people in ways I never dreamed about. As you continue on, you'll find more of my story throughout the book. One thing I can tell you is that I decided that I didn't want to be average. So I ask you, please, as you go on your journey, do that little bit extra. Don't strive to be average; there are already enough people in that line.

GENE K. J. KOPCZYK

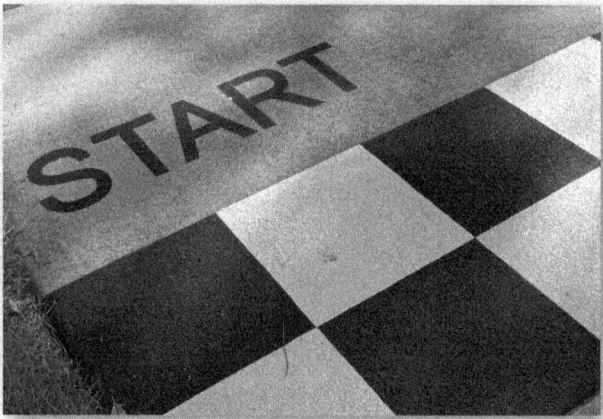

You don't have to be great to get started. You have to get started to be great!

# CHAPTER 1

## I WAS JUST THINKING

If you don't ask the answer is always no.

LET'S BEGIN HERE...RIGHT here, with your thoughts. It's important to understand that everything that is and everything that will be began as a thought in someone's mind. Understand we're not talking about trees and grass and things in nature; however, those things were also a thought that came to be. I'm talking about all tangible, man-made items that we use every day. Understand that at some point in time they didn't exist.

That's right; there was a time when the light bulb that we take for granted now didn't exist. But I bet the first thing you do when you enter a dark room is…what? You reach for the light switch, which sends power to the light bulb and illuminates the room. In fact, it has become so second nature to us that we get angry when the bulb is blown out and doesn't work at our command.

When was the last time you stopped to appreciate the automobile? You know, the thing we climb into and entrust with our lives as we travel here and there. We simply get in, turn the key, listen for the engine to hum, put it in gear, and go—never stopping to think what might have happened if the car had never been a thought in someone's mind. Can you imagine taking that weekend getaway on foot? I bet you wouldn't walk too far from home.

I bring this up because your thoughts are where everything begins. When you begin to understand how your thoughts impact everything you do, think, or even feel, you may start to understand why it's important to be careful about what thoughts you let go in and out of your mind. In fact, everything you are, have done, will do, and will say is the sum total of your thoughts.

While science has yet to discover exactly how thoughts come in and out of the mind, it can tell us which part of the brain functions when we are having specific types of thoughts. Scientists have been able to map out which hemisphere of the brain is active when someone is having a creative thought or is angry. Believe me when I tell you that there is nothing that science has built that can keep up with the human train of thought. We are by far the most advanced thinking machines that exist on the planet, to the extent that we have ventured out to the moon and even other planets. The problem is that most of us don't understand how the brain works or even think about it. We just kind of go through life taking for granted that sitting right on top of our shoulders is the most powerful problem-solving machine—a machine that humanity has never figured out.

One of the problems with our thoughts is that they run so deep, we don't know how to explain them sometimes. The mind is so complex that it's impossible for us to understand. Take, for example, the existence of your subconscious mind. I promise it exists, and I can prove it. This is a part of the mind that science really doesn't understand at all, even though scientists know it's there. It functions in conjunction with your conscious mind. For example, have you ever been driving to work and gotten lost in thinking about the day or what needs to be done when you get home? Maybe about what you are going to do this weekend, or how great the vacation is going to be next month? The next thing you know, you're reaching down to turn off the ignition because you've arrived at your destination. Somehow you actually drove yourself to work, school, or the store, but you have no conscious recollection of how you arrived there. That, my friend, was your subconscious at work. While you were lost in thought, your subconscious took over and essentially did the boring, mundane job of getting you where you needed to go without you having to consciously put much effort into making it there. Your subconscious literally caused you to steer the car, change lanes, use your turn signal, make turns, and park safely at your destination with little to no effort on your part. The important fact about the subconscious that we often overlook is that we can put it to work for us whenever we like to.

We literally limit our potential and ourselves by our thoughts. Sometimes it's not even our *own* thoughts that limit us. Think about it and you'll find that, throughout your life, many other people have shared their thoughts with you and that you may have taken in these pieces of advice. They were not yours, but somehow they manifested themselves as your thoughts and became your reality.

Take the old pattern of thought that Mom and Dad probably told you. When you were a child, they nurtured your creative side and told you that you could be anything and could do anything that you wanted to do—"The sky's the limit." The funny part is that they were absolutely correct; there was nothing that they could have told you that would have been more absolutely truthful! For some reason, though, at some point, we stop believing that it's true, that ultimately we don't have the ability to do anything. Why? It's simple, really. What you'll find is that the people you love and who love you, the ones you deeply admire and care about, have the most influence on you and your thoughts. See, if most of you are like me, eventually those very same people who once told you that you could do anything tell you to "get your head of out the clouds" and "buckle down." Sometimes you even start to hear early on—sometimes even from the school counselor—"To make it in this world, you have to work hard, go to school, get good grades, get into a good college, and get a good job." The problem is that we accept this—these thoughts that don't belong to us—and we begin to let go of our own thoughts, our imagination, and our dreams.

You'll find that almost 99 percent of the time, it was someone we loved and respected who changed our thoughts so that we believed what he or she thought was best. The point here is not to place blame on anyone, but to understand that these individuals embedded this thought pattern in you because that's what they knew; they had been out in the world and had learned a few things, and they didn't want you to make the same mistakes they had made. They didn't want to see you get hurt. So they took what others had told them, and what they had seen, and implanted a new set of thoughts in you. So where do you think they heard all this advice that they are now giving to you? That's right, they heard this is in the same manner that you did, from someone they loved and respected.

Most people believe that anyone who loves you would never want to hurt you, and this is right. But one problem is that this line of thinking only leads you in one direction. What is that, you ask? It puts you on the path to being really good at living someone else's dream for that person. "Impossible," you say, "that's not true." But I have been to many places in my life, and I have seen many things that most won't ever get to see, and one thing I see repeatedly is people living someone else's dream.

Take the autoworker, for example. I use this example because I come from a long line of autoworkers, as my grandfather, father, aunt, and in-laws are all from Michigan. I am very proud to say that. At one point, the automotive industry provided great lives for many workers in this country, and it helped the United States become the leader in many fields. However, if we take a good look at the typical autoworker today, we'll find that this person feels trapped. Usually his or her opinion is that he or she is stuck where he or she is and sees no way out. Why is that? I mean, autoworkers have good incomes, a stable job, and good health care, and, depending on when they were hired, the company will even give them a pension when they retire for the years of service they've put in. So why does the assembler feel trapped? Because he or she is living someone else's dream and not his or her own; he or she is going to a place he or she doesn't want to be and, a lot of the time, is working with people he or she doesn't get along with. It's unfortunate, but in every job I have had, and among all the people I have spoken with, I have found that there are personality conflicts in the workplace. Some people are just so negative about everything that no matter how nice you try to be to everyone, these negative people will end up despising you, sometimes for being "too nice." You tend to find this is occasionally worse in the factory-type setting of the automotive job because, in a sense, your office is the ten to fourteen feet of space immediately next to the person who has an issue with you, and there's nowhere to retreat to.

The worker at that plant knows innately that he or she is capable of so much more than showing up to a place for eight to twelve hours a day and doing the same exact thing over and over again for thirty or more years. It reminds me of the old Greek legend of Atlas, who was punished by having to push a boulder uphill for all eternity. Wow, that really sounds exciting, doesn't it? I promise you that all of these people heard the same refrain: "Work hard, get good grades, get into a good school, and get a good job." The other thing I am absolutely confident of is that they will tell their offspring the same thing, and the cycle will start over again. Those same destructive thoughts that kept them going to jobs they couldn't stand will infect another generation, not because these workers want to be cruel to the next generation, but because it's what they know. Unfortunately, a lot of dreams and goals will be lost forever. And that doesn't really sound like too much of a dream life, does it?

My point in all of this is that your thoughts are very real things, and they lay the foundations for everything that has happened and will happen in your life. Your thoughts can be awesome and can actually become tangible goods and services that people use every day—or they can lead you down a path to having a life of pain and regret, and I promise you, that's a mighty bitter path. Imagine you were on your deathbed; what do you think your thoughts would be? Do you really think that you would wish you had spent more time at the factory? Or maybe that you could've just watched a little more TV? Sounds ridiculous, doesn't it?

This is why you must decide to pick your thoughts carefully. You would be amazed at how easily you can direct your thoughts—especially those of your subconscious. For example, say to yourself, "I don't feel good." Did you feel that? Now wait about ten seconds and say, "I feel great." Did you feel that? It's just a small sample of how thoughts affect you. Keep in mind that I've planted those thoughts in your head, so make sure you control your own thoughts so that nothing can stop you from accomplishing anything that you want to do with the precious time that has been given to you. Be aware of whom you're speaking to and what people are saying to you, so that you don't have someone else's thoughts planted into your mind. Now, stop thinking about zebras. See, it works!

Once you begin to focus on your thoughts and how they affect you and your thinking, you'll really begin to pay more attention to what you're listening to. I have heard people say, "If you like what you have, keep doing what you're doing, and you'll keep getting what you're getting." That's very true, but understand that it was your thinking that caused you to start doing what you are doing and getting what you are getting right now. So I would say instead that if you like what you're getting, keep thinking the way you're thinking. But if you don't like what you're getting right now, you're going to have to change your stinkin' thinkin'!

# CHAPTER 2

# BELIEVING IN YOURSELF

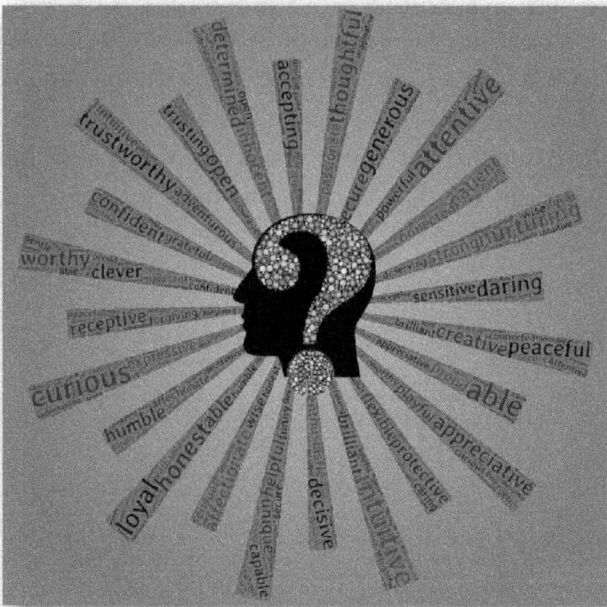

If you don't go after what you want, you'll never have it.

THERE IS AN important point to be made here, which is this: most people think that they believe in themselves. But there's something confusing about these people's lives: these same people are not living their dream. They are the ones who get up and go to the same job day in and day out, over and over again, all the while complaining that they dislike the boss and that they can't stand Monday mornings. They can usually be seen running from the building come Friday at quitting time, yelling, "Thank God it's Friday." At some point in life, people begin to become confused about what "believing in yourself" really means. They seem to think that believing in themselves means believing they exist. While that is one way to look at it, it's not truly believing in oneself.

Let's take a walk back in time to when you truly believed in yourself. You may ask, "How would you know when I believed in myself and when I didn't?" The simple answer is this: when you were young. You may not exactly remember, but when you were young, you believed in yourself with every fiber of your being. "How do I know that?" you ask.

Well, when you were born, much like the rest of us, you were helpless. It's interesting to me that, of all the creatures on earth, humans are the only ones who are born absolutely helpless. Think of any other species on the planet. Fish, from the second they are born, know how to swim. When they hatch, sea turtles know to scramble back to the ocean and know how to swim. And within minutes of being born, a newborn calf will stand and go in search of its mother and begin to feed.

Humans, on the other hand, are born completely empty, just waiting to be filled with sights, sounds, and information. Unless Mom and Dad, or someone is there to take care of us, how long would we last? I would venture to say maybe a few hours, and at most, only a few days. However, we are nurtured by those who love us, and we survive. Eventually we decide that lying on only our bellies or backs just doesn't cut it for us, so we begin to try and flip over so we can see more of the world. Once we accomplish that, we discover that everyone else seems to be moving around, and we want to move with them. So we eventually figure out how to turn back over. Little by little, we place one arm and leg forward, and then the other, and we repeat this process until we can crawl. At some point, we decide that crawling is nice, but it doesn't get us around quite fast enough. So we grab on to the table or the chair and pull ourselves up. Slowly and unsteadily, we place one foot in front of the other and begin to take steps forward. After a little while of failing, and failing and more failing, we are running through the house, and Mom and Dad can hardly keep up with us.

Why? Why did we try to accomplish something that we didn't understand and had no clue of how to even begin to do, or that we didn't even know our bodies were capable of doing? Quite honestly, we failed at walking how many thousands of times before we were able to do it? So why didn't we just quit after the first or second time we fell down? We learned to walk because we saw someone else doing it, and at that moment our little brains were developed enough that they created the thought that if someone else could do it, so could we. If we were fortunate, everyone was excited to see us walk, and that helped, but the other thing we had going for us at the time was that we didn't understand language.

Yes, it sounds funny to say, but it's the truth. We didn't understand what people around us were saying, and so their words had no effect on us or our determination to stand and walk. How far do you think you would have walked if you understood the language first and people were telling you that you couldn't do it and you should give up? At that point, the only thing we had was a pure sense of belief in ourselves. I'm not sure that anyone ever reaches that state of belief again in his or her life. Don't get me wrong, some get very close, but that, my friend, was a point in your life when all you had was belief in you.

So why tell you this?

What difference does it make?

How can it help you?

This is the point of the journey that most people stop at. They get an idea or a notion about something, but they don't act on it. How many times have you thought about doing something and talked yourself out of it? Most of the time we become our own worst enemies by doubting ourselves and speaking negatively to ourselves. Do you ever think about how you talk to yourself? The fact is that sometimes we speak so poorly to ourselves that if we had friends who spoke to us that way, we would stop talking to them. But we continue on doing just this to ourselves, and thus the self-doubt and negative talk continue until we somehow buy into the idea that we can't do it, and we ultimately come up with every excuse for why we can't.

Sometimes when we stop, it's because we have talked to someone else, a friend or loved one, who tells us how hard it's going to be, or how much money it's going to cost. Then we get upset a couple years later when we see that someone else got our idea and ran with it. Now that person has the time and money to pursue things that he or she wants to do and live in the manner he or she wants to live.

What do you think would have happened if every time you got an idea about something in your life, you pursued it with the same tenacity that you pursued walking? Do you think anyone could have stopped you from reaching your true potential, from achieving any goal that you set? My guess is that had you done that, you would have found your passion and would be living your dream. Unfortunately, we don't do this; we quit on ourselves and settle for the comfort of what we know and can physically touch. I would argue that most people shouldn't be called "grown-ups," but "given-ups," because that's exactly what most of them have done. At some point, we reach a comfort zone and lose our belief in ourselves. So what's the way back?

Get out of your comfort zone; the land of familiarity is for the dead. Let me say it this way. Most people die at twenty-five and wait until seventy-five to be buried.

I know what you're thinking: "But it will be hard?"

Yes.

"Will I struggle?"

Yes.

"What if I fail?"

You will fail many times. Unfortunately, the only pattern that seems to work is dream, struggle, victory. Without a test, there can be no testimony. Look at anyone who has ever done anything worthwhile in his or her life. I promise that this person will not tell you about how easy it was for him or her. Life is hard, and there will be pain. You'll find that you will suffer two things: the pain of regret and the pain of disappointment. So if you're going to go through the struggle and pain anyway, you may as well get something out of it. I say, get the life you want out of it. The problem is that you are struggling with the decision to do it—that's really all it is. It's one little decision. It's easy to do, but also it's easy *not* to do; that is the problem. Growth is painful, and change is painful, but you'll find that nothing is as painful as staying stuck somewhere you don't belong.

I had a friend tell me a great story the other day about his son. The boy had been working at a place he thought he liked and enjoyed, but after a few months, he found that he really didn't like it all that much anymore, and it was really more of a pain. But the job paid him pretty well, so he kept going in it. Sound familiar: the old "job waltz"? You know it well; all of us have tried it at some point. You know how, in this kind of job, you'll do just enough not to get fired, and the employer pays you just enough to keep you from leaving. Anyway, through some circumstances, the boy got fired. He came home and told his father about it; the son was very upset at having been fired. His dad was telling me this part of the story, and I had to stop him.

I said, "Wait a minute—didn't you tell me he had begun to seriously dislike that job?"

My friend said, "Yes."

I said, "Well, then, what is he upset about? They didn't fire him, they set him free. Now he can go pursue something he would be more fulfilled doing!"

You see, when you find your passion and begin to work on it diligently, you will feel fulfilled. The simple fact is that there are things that are out of our control that will push us in certain directions. Call it the universe if you will. In this case, if the universe had not moved so that this man's son got out of that job, he would have become more comfortable over time, and he would have lost his belief in himself, that he is capable of so much more. In the end, he would have spent most of his time hating what he was doing and where he was going.

You have to make a conscious decision to believe in yourself in your abilities. The more you doubt yourself, the more belief you will lose in yourself—this doubt is just like a cancer growing in your mind. So I say, get it out now. If you're reading this book, you have already figured out that things are not going along as you would like. Now that you have that figured out, zap that cancer out of your head for good. You have already beat millions of sperm cells to be here. You proved your worth just by being born. You'll never have to face those odds again. So why did you stop believing in yourself?

The nice part is that you can start again. You see, this is truly *your* life. You are in control of it. You're the one writing the script, so if you don't like it, change it; make it into what you want it to be. You have always had the option to start a new chapter and change the way your story flows and ends. Here's what I can tell you without a doubt: when you decide to rewrite your life, you will feel a power like you have never felt before. It will feel a little uneasy at first, but as things start to come together and you begin to see your thoughts becoming reality, you will not want to be stopped, and no excuse will be good enough. You will be a force to be reckoned with!

# CHAPTER 3

## IGNORING NEGATIVITY

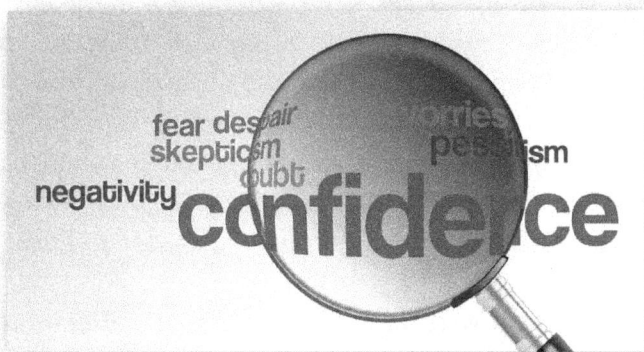

No really means Next Opportunity.

I REALIZE THAT the chapter title is almost always easier said than done. There are so many people out there in the world just waiting to tell you how everything *can't* be done. Even worse, you'll be the first to tell *you* how it can't be done. From the minute you show up on the planet, you are faced with negativity. You just got here, and the first thing they can think to do is smack you on the bottom. I think this is meant to be your first lesson in what you will have to contend with. So, just know that you're going to have to take some hits in life. Now, let's take a look at exactly whom we have to contend with.

When you start to look at how you can ignore negativity, you have to look at how you talk to yourself. Some of us actually carry on conversations with ourselves in our minds, and sometimes, if we're alone with the mirror, we will add sound effects. What types of things do you say to yourself? Do you tell yourself how good you look, what a great day you're going to have, how good you feel today?

I'm guessing that, like most people, you probably get up telling yourself how bad you feel, and you continue this fantastic conversation into all the following topics: how you don't have the energy and strength to go to work today; how much you would really just like to go back to bed or just stay in bed; how much your body aches; how mean the guy in the next cubicle or on the line is; or how much that guy on the dock in shipping doesn't like you and you don't know why, you never did anything to him. Does any of this sound familiar? Do you know anyone like this, or is this you? Do you stand around the water cooler or coffee pot grumbling about how bad you have it, while the others in the band claim to have it worse? Do you do this to play the "my pain is worse than your pain" game for a while?

You see, the negative things you say to yourself affect you way more than anything anyone else could possibly say to you. Why? Because your mind—both the subconscious and conscious parts—is always listening! The trade-off to this fact is that a negative comment will require six positive comments to wipe it out based on a study done at Berkley. You have to realize that sometimes the only good conversation you might be able to have is the one you have with yourself. So how can you feel good, have a great day, or have confidence in your appearance or your mental state if you don't tell yourself positive things? Understand that every day, and in everything you say, you have to make a conscience choice to be, do, and say positive things. Is it easy? No, it's hard. You might as well get it in your mind right now that "easy" is not an option, and it never will be. So now that you know that, it's hard just decide to do it hard!

There is so much negativity in the world that will try to crush the positive out of you. People who are negative or engage in negative, depressing talk love to be around others who do the same. I'm sure you have heard the old sayings "misery loves company" and "birds of a feather flock together." Well, these clichés are true, so start paying attention to the people you associate with. Listen to how they talk, and try to interject some positive into the conversation and see their reaction. Most of the time they will either roll their eyes at you or try to engage you in an argument to prove how wrong you are. So work on getting your mind right, and your actions will follow. Understand that negative talk and behaviors are just habits that you have created over time. The nice part about a habit is that it can be broken; you don't have to live in a negative environment. All you have to do is choose to make better choices over and over again until these choices become your new habits.

One of the things I suggest you do is to engage in positive conversation the people whom you're around most, and see what their reaction is. For example, if the weather has been nice lately, you might comment on that—I mean, really, who doesn't like nice weather? More importantly, it is an experience that you and the other person have shared, both of you having been outside at some point. Even if it's been raining, you can find something positive in it: maybe the rain will help with the garden or how dry the grass was getting. Another idea is to bring up a mutual acquaintance and see what the person's reaction is. Or, perhaps you might give a person a compliment and see how he or she reacts. Take note of this reaction, and do your best to avoid people or things that are negative. I promise, it will be difficult to keep all of them away, and a lot of them will blame you and ask, "What's wrong with you?" as if you have some disease. So keep in mind that through this process, you're going to lose some people who you thought were friends. Oh, and they will blame you for why they don't talk to you anymore; they will run around telling everyone how you've changed and they "just don't get you anymore." By the way, that's another great characteristic in negative people—it's never their fault. It's always someone or something else who did this or that who caused them to be and act this way. Nonsense—it is them and was them all along; they just don't want to accept the fact that they are in control of their life and that they make the decision to be how they are.

When I began my journey, I finally accepted that the reason things were not going well for me and had not worked out for me was that I had not done the things that were necessary to get the results I wanted. It was hard for me to admit that I was the one at fault for how my life was going and that, if I wanted someone to rescue me, I had better look in the mirror. So I got busy doing the things that needed to be done, and in the process I looked around to find that all these people who I thought were friends were gone because I didn't agree with everything they said. I didn't care for their opinions about how stomping on others was how people should treat each other. To these former "friends," I became a bad person because I was no longer following the crowd. I eventually looked around and found I was down to one friend. He had watched me go through this change. I had had two real friends, but one had passed away while I was finding out who I was, and I was given the great honor of speaking about and eulogizing him. But that one friend I still had would tell me over and over how proud he was of me, how proud he was to call me his friend, and it was enough for me to know that I was headed in the right direction.

My problem was that following the crowd had never gotten me close to anything I wanted to achieve in life. The crowd goes toward what's popular, and not what's right for the individual person. So, in following the crowd, you really have no idea where you are being led to. Then, when you get there and look around, you tend to find out you're not where you want to be. What makes it worse is that there's no do-over; you can't rewind time and try again. So my suggestion to you is to take a good look at the crowd you're following, and make sure it is heading in a direction that you want to go.

# CHAPTER 4

## USING NEGATIVITY TO YOUR ADVANTAGE

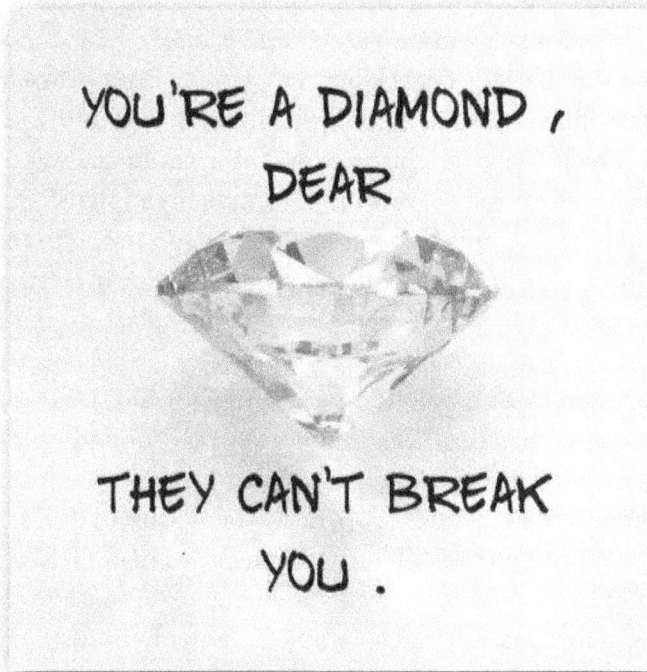

YOU'RE A DIAMOND, DEAR

THEY CAN'T BREAK YOU.

Let them criticize who they think you are.

So NOW THAT we have covered how negativity can creep into your mind and erode your thoughts, and how you should try to ignore it, I think it's a good idea to talk about how to use it to help you. That's right, you can actually use negativity to help yourself. Once you can easily identify it when it comes after you, and you know for sure it's going to come after you, then you have the opportunity to decide how to use it in your life. You can make a conscious decision to let it affect you, drive you, and motivate you—or you can simply not let it bother you.

How do we start to make these decisions about how to use negativity? It's called "practice." You actually have to work at it. Just like anything else, when you identify the problem, then you must take the steps to direct and correct it. So when a person says something negative to you, you then have to process it to figure out what to do with the comment. You may decide to just let it roll off because maybe the person saying that thing is not doing all that great or is having a bad day and is looking for someone to get down in the dumps with him or her. Or you may find yourself in a situation where someone says something negative to you and you'll have to decide how much you value this person's information anyway. If you find he or she is usually negative, this may be a time to let that comment slide off you. I mean, really think about it. If the person trying to tell you how your something is no good and that person is standing in front of you with his or her nothing, how much value can you really place on the comment?

Look around right now at the people in your life. Make a list on paper if you need to. Just think about how they react and interact with you, and the types of things they say to you. Now, go down the list and as you think about how the person is when he or she is around you. If you're being honest, you can already identify the negative people. No, they don't get special credit for being a family member or because you've known them for so many years. The fact is, these individuals just might be the people who are holding you back because they are family members or you've know them for so many years.

I can tell you this: I have had people come into my life at different points in my life, people whose only purpose seemed to be to try and be as negative as they could toward me. I remember that my junior-high-school counselor actually told my parents that they were "wasting their time" with me, that I was "not worth the effort," and that he was tired of "wasting the school's resources on a lost cause"—the school should really just let me "sink or swim." Now, I'm not going to tell you his name was Tom Bently, but I will tell you there is a reason that I remember his name after all these years. When he said all these horrible things about me, it ignited a fire in me that to this day has not been put out. I remember thinking, *I'll show you. I'll be so successful that you'll have to take that statement back.* Understand that when he said that statement about me, it hurt, and I had to make a choice. I could agree with him, and join the party of "See, Mom and Dad, I told you I'm just no good." Or I could start making some better choices and work harder—even if I had to outwork everyone else, I could make it. My parents always told me I could be anything and do anything I wanted. All I can say is, thank God that I chose to believe them and not Mr. Bently. But there's still a part of me that wonders if Tom Bently identified that which would drive me and used it to motivate me. I can say at this point in my life that I will give him the benefit of the doubt. We'll say he gambled on the idea that his statement would motivate the kid with ADD to drive himself to become more.

So let's look at another turning point in my life. I should probably tell you that I come from what I call a split family. I have four older siblings; three of them are from my mother's first marriage, and one is from her marriage to my father. When we were young, the three oldest children, those from my mother's first marriage, took great pride in trying to convince me and my sister that we were adopted children and so our parents didn't really care about us the way they cared about them. As a child, I didn't know any better, and to some extent, it didn't bother me. I didn't really know what they were talking about and really didn't care; I just wanted to play. I remember asking my father about this information when I was about four or five years old. He explained to me that I was his and my mother's child as well, as was my sister, and he had adopted the other three children my mother had because they asked to be adopted and have the same last name as me and my sister. I suppose he assumed I had overheard my mother and him talking and thought I was confused about the adoption. He still made sure to instill in me that even though he had adopted the other three, they were still very much my siblings, as we all had the same mother.

Unfortunately, though, my sister, who is six years older than I am, understood what the older three were trying to sell, and she bought into it. She never asked my parents until many, many years later, and some of the damage that it caused in her relationships was not going to be undone anytime soon once she learned the truth. My sister had to go to several therapists and ended up with a very bad inferiority complex. She very well may still be seeing a therapist today. If she is, I sincerely hope she's getting the help she needs. One therapist eventually convinced her that everyone in our family was bad, and if she would just leave us all, she would be better off—so one day she did just that. No, this doesn't mean that all therapists are bad; this particular one was giving opinions when he or she should have been helping my sister find answers; or it's entirely possible that my sister fabricated the lie that a therapist had given her this advice because she thought that leaving would be best for her. Either way, I hope she is doing well.

So I tell you this to draw a parallel between the two people who were exposed to the same circumstances. One had what she thought was a little more knowledge about the situation. The other had significantly less knowledge about the situation. But in reality, my sister, thinking she truly understood what was going on, bought into a phony idea that we were adopted and unlovable. Because of this, she lost so many years fighting with these types of thoughts in her mind, trying to reason it out and understand why anyone would treat her in this manner. She lost a lot of good relationships and had several bad relationships. So much of her life was unfortunately wasted in trying to cope with and figure out why a sibling would do something like this.

So let's fast-forward to later down the road. I found myself working at a restaurant as a busboy. One evening I noticed a name in the reservations book that was the same as my eldest half sister's married name—yes, one of the ones who tried to convince me that I was adopted. It appeared that she and her family were coming in for dinner that evening. So I had the hostess notify me of where they were seated. As it turns out, it was in fact my half sister and her family, which included her husband and my niece and nephew. I approached her table; greeted them; said hello and that I hoped they were doing well and would enjoy their meal; and went on about my work. A few moments later, I was told my half sister wanted to see me in the vestibule.

When I approached my sister, she looked upset and immediately began be berate me. She asked, "Who do you think you are to ruin our dinner?" She continued to get louder and louder, and more irate.

When I suggested she calm down, it just angered her more, until eventually, her final words to me were: "You're shit, you were raised in shit, and all you'll ever be is shit."

I stood there with my jaw to the ground, not understanding what I had done to deserve this verbal attack. In my mind I remember thinking, *You have no idea who I am and what I am capable of. You never took any interest in me, and now, after all these years, this is all you can say to me.*

At this point, she had gone back to her seat, and she began packing up her family. As I turned to go back to work, I noticed that there were several people who had come through the door behind me and were waiting to be seated. I remember the looks on their faces as they just stared back at me.

So I said, "She really didn't like the specials tonight. I would stay away from them if I were you."

Everyone there burst into laughter, and I went back to work.

Now, at this point I had to make a choice. I could choose to believe what my half sister had said to me, or I could prove her wrong—not that she would ever know, but I would know, and that was what was most important. I had to decide that I was not going to believe the venom that my half sister wanted to run around spitting on people. I was already struggling to overcome an inferiority complex that I had most of my life due to the way my siblings had treated me: My older half sister would so desperately try to convince everyone of her false statements. My half brother would whup my behind on an almost-daily basis. My next-oldest half sister, on her eighteenth birthday, just up and left home, and it wasn't long until she never spoke to any of us again. And finally, my actual sister got so caught up in our older half sister's nonsense that she couldn't find a reason or way out.

I once heard a man say that someone's opinion of you does not have to become your reality. I don't think I have ever heard a more true statement, so I'll write it again: someone's opinion of you does not have to become your reality. We are made by those who love us and by those who refuse to love us. So I made a choice to not believe my half sister. After all, she never took much interest in my life, so how could she possibly form this opinion? I admit, the fact she had left home when I was young and we never had much of a relationship made my decision easier. But I still had to make a choice to not buy into her lies. In the same way, you should think more highly of yourself and not buy into whatever other people say about you.

You have to be careful of whom you take advice from. I'm sure you've heard the expression "One bad apple can spoil a bunch." Well, there's another one that says, "One negative person can ruin your whole life." I decided I was going to show everyone in my family that all their opinions of me were not going to become my reality. I began to do things that I thought would help me to improve myself. I had figured out that, in all honesty, the only real guarantee we have in life is that we don't get out alive.

While you're here, people are going are going to criticize you; we have to come to terms with this fact. They do this for many different reasons. Some of the time, they will criticize you because they're small-minded—they don't see the bigger picture in life. I think that a lot of these types of people don't want to see life on a bigger scale because they're afraid they'll have to live up to this view. Another reason is that they may have tunnel vision. You may have heard several versions of this attitude: "I can't do it," "This is all I'm good at," and—my favorite— "I'm only human," as if being human gives us the excuse to somehow be less than what we can be. Quite honestly, if these people never take the time to learn something new or become interested in a different way of doing something, then they are right—they have reached the peak of what they can do or will do, because they have not tried to stretch their minds. So always understand that when a person opens his or her mouth to you, that is his or her thought and opinion, and it does not have to become your reality.

CHAPTER 5

# ELIMINATING SELF-DOUBT

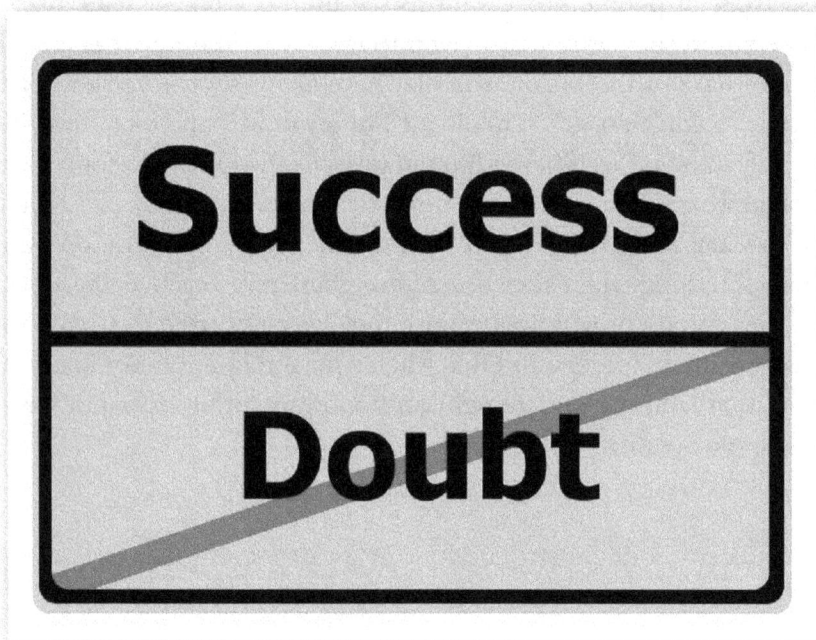

Just because it took you longer than others doesn't mean you failed.

SELF-DOUBT IS WHAT I like to call the "cancer of the mind." Unfortunately, there is no surgery, drug, or treatment that can remove it. You have to battle this poor type of thinking consciously in your mind until you eliminate it. You have probably developed the habit because, at some point in your life, you wanted to do something, and someone you loved or admired told you that you were not good enough to do that. It was then that the seeds of self-doubt were planted. You began to measure everything by that standard. The worst part about it is that it was not your standard. It was someone else's standard of themselves, and because this person felt he or she couldn't do it, he or she told you that you couldn't either, and you began to use their statement as a measuring device in your mind. This is one of the most destructive habits that we get into and that you must overcome. This will paralyze you from being able to do anything. It's that inner conversation in your mind that tells you those little things like: "Well, it probably won't work anyway," "I don't know enough about that to make it work," "I don't have the resources to put it together," and "They will probably laugh at me and tell me it's no good."

We've all had these types of thoughts or said these types of things to ourselves at one point or another. So let me ask you: do think the Wright brothers were the first people to invent the airplane? This is what someone told you, but it's not true. Some historians point out that there was actually an airplane invented by Gustav Weisskopf (Whitehead) from Germany before the Wright brothers ever tried to get their plane off the ground. Whether or not Weisskopf did design a plane before the Wright brothers, conventional thinking said man was not meant to fly. You don't think the Wright brothers were told the plane would never work? You better believe they were told it wouldn't work. More importantly, do you know what kept them going after this? They finally saw their creation lift off the ground for a few seconds. That was all it took. They knew if they could get it off the ground for a few seconds, and then a few minutes, that they could make it stay in the air as long as it needed to. Because they just kept going, the world would never be the same again. They came through this process of invention, and afterward the world would never be the same again. Now, what if they had listened to the people who said, "It will never work. You'll never get it off the ground"?

Now, the story goes that when Gustav Weisskopf, who had created the plane years earlier, was asked why he didn't complete the project, he said a colleague had seen his invention and told him that it was impractical and would never become useful. The self-doubt sank in, and he became too afraid to try. I greatly admire the Wright brothers for their courage to face their fear and criticism. It also doesn't hurt that I too always wanted to fly, but I always thought you either went to college or you went to flight school. Luckily, I found out I was wrong; I could still go learn how to fly. It's really a great story, but I'll save those details for another time. But I am happy to report that on December 26, 2015, the Federal Aviation Administration issued me my private-pilot license. See, humanity truly was intended to fly!

Fortunately for a lot of travelers today, the Wright Brothers chose to push past the criticisms and fear of failure. At some point in your life, you too will begin to look around at the circumstances that you are in, and you will have to make a choice. You will know this point because prior to it, you will have been cruising through life on a form of autopilot, never feeling like you have accomplished anything or that you are truly happy with where you are. Most of the time, our instincts will kick in to remove us from whatever is trying to harm us. Sometimes we don't know which way to go, and we'll stay in a bad situation for a while, hoping that it passes. Then again, sometimes we choose to accept it as the norm and just stay mired down in it. I think that's why Henry David Thoreau said, "Most people lead lives of quiet desperation." This happens because we don't have the confidence in ourselves to create a new set of circumstances.

I once read a book by John Powell called *Why Am I Afraid to Tell You Who I Am?* Throughout this book, the author answers his central question, but one of the most powerful statements I thought he made was a very simple answer to his question: "Why am I afraid to tell you who I am? Because you might not like me and that's really all I have." The book did a great job explaining where our self-doubt might begin to form. I had never thought of what the author described, and it was a real eye-opener for me. We all know that our parents love and care for us as much as they can. But did you ever stop to think that some of even the good advice they give us could be perceived and warped in our minds into a toxic and self-doubting message? Think of all the things your parents or loved ones ever told you—and I mean all the positive things, the things you even today know you should do, as well as any negative things that someone might have said to you that would cause you to feel self-doubt.

As I read the words John Powell had written, I could not believe that this had never occurred to me. How many times in your life has your mom, dad, or other loved one said to you, as you were leaving, that you should "be careful"? If I had to guess, I would say that as a child I heard this phrase about a million times a month. It seemed like I was always being told to "be careful." What I came to learn was that this could be a very negative thing to say to a person, though the result does depend on the person and his or her current mental attitude. The underlying meaning behind "be careful" can be interpreted to mean that you are not able to handle anything or everything that is outside in the world, and so severe harm may come to you. In reality, though, the speaker may just be asking you not to take risks or chances so you don't get hurt or harmed, because if something were to happen to you, he or she could not handle it.

So the person who tells you anything unfortunately passes along to you his or her own lack of trust in himself or herself, his or her fear that he or she can't handle a thing or situation. With this, we begin to pick up a lack of self-confidence, and in a distinct way, we begin to fear everything that may be waiting for us out in the world. It takes hold of our subconscious and begins to direct our every line of thought and every decision that we make. To not take chances, we don't take any risks, because we have to "be careful" so that we don't get into harm's way.

The bigger concern you should have with this line of thought is that only trying to make choices based on others' opinions doesn't get you where you want to be. Now, I'm not in any way suggesting that you should cross against the light, never use your turn signal, or speed because the car can go that fast. What I am saying is that, in your heart of hearts, you know what you should be doing. Typically, when you try to make a choice or decision in life, your mind automatically lets that self-doubt set in, and you think you might not be able to handle it, so you either shy away from what you really want to do or you don't make any decision. By the way, let's just cover this now—deciding not to decide is in itself a decision. So don't pump yourself up thinking you have outsmarted anyone or anything by simply deciding not to decide.

If you continue to go through life doubting yourself all the time, you will end up with a life of mediocrity. You will have no choice but to settle for whatever anyone will give you, instead of what you really want. So you will have made a choice to try to safely make it to your grave. Does that even make any sense? Can you imagine anyone trying to set that as a goal when asked what he or she wants to do with his or her life: "Well, I just want to tiptoe to my grave and get there nice and safe"? I can't even imagine wanting to take the journey of this life, the only one you have, and not make the most out of it.

At some point, you will realize the hard, cold reality is that self-doubt is a trick. It's a trick that people use to make sure you don't get ahead of where they are. They try to convince you that you can't do anything either, or that it would be too risky for you to try anything, or that you might get hurt. By telling you these things, they keep the flames of self-doubt burning. Understand that your heart will lead you to where you want to go, whereas your mind will lead you to your fears. It's the heart that will help you eliminate self-doubt. It's your heart that wanted that girlfriend, boyfriend, wife, or husband. It's the heart that wanted that new car, or that new job, or that new business.

The mind, in contrast, will tell you all the possible bad outcomes, all the reasons why things might not work out for you. You've had this conversation in your mind, I know you have. Right? The mind will trick you into believing all of the following doubts: "You're not good enough." "What if he or she doesn't like me?" "What if I get rejected, or I get laughed at" The mind will, almost every time, lead you to your fears. Why? Because that's how it has been programmed almost all your life. During that time, it has created a great wall of self-doubt that you carry around with you, and anytime your heart wants to try something, your mind forces you to take a good long look at how big and tall and long that great wall of self-doubt is.

This is where most people give up. But not you, not this time. I can tell you a little secret: if, while you're standing there, looking at that wall in your mind, you just throw your heart over it, the body and mind will follow. What the mind doesn't understand is that it cannot function without the heart. So if you throw it over the wall, the heart creates desire, and the mind solves the problems. They work in conjunction, but you have to learn to trust your heart for the mind and body to follow. It really is that simple; they just can't survive without each other. The nice part is the mind doesn't know that when the heart makes the decision, the mind has lost control and can now only solve the problem of how to get what the heart wants.

Another way to look at it is that the mind, to some extent, is lazy. This is why it shows you all of the problems and reasons why it's too hard, and why you should go back and not do it. What the mind is really doing is trying to figure out how to get out of work. On some level, the mind knows that when you throw your heart over the wall, it has to go to work to figure out how to get over, under, around, or through that wall. So if it can talk you into stopping before you even start, then it's already solved the problem of having to start working on getting what the heart wants. At that point, the mind can shut down and go back on cruise control. It is exactly at this point that you need to throw your heart over the wall.

Think about all the problems you have ever faced in your life. Eventually your mind solved them for you, didn't it? Of course it did, because that's all it knows how to do; it calculates and solves problems. It is, without a doubt, the greatest computer for problem-solving that has ever existed on the planet. Nothing man-made even comes close to the problems that the mind can solve. Always remember that the heart will lead you to your passion, and the mind will lead you to your fear. Choose to listen to your heart.

# CHAPTER 6

## CHANGING YOUR THINKING

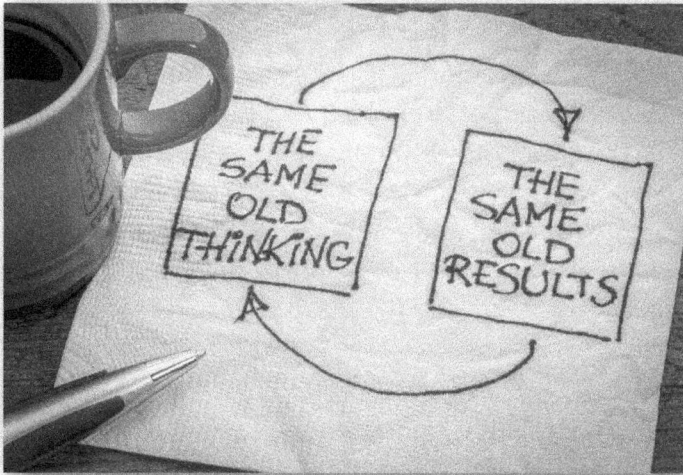

If you want something different you have think differently.

THE HARDEST THING you may have to do now is learn to change your stinkin' thinkin'. Yeah, I said it. *Change*—sometimes it's almost considered a bad word. In fact, when you say it, some people will look at you as if you have just uttered the worst four-letter word you could think of at them. The ancient Greek philosopher Heraclitus said, "The only thing that is constant is change." He is right; as badly as you may want to hold on to something, the environment your in will change around you. There is no way to stop it.

One of the problems that we face with change is to change our thinking to fit with the new parameters that we must work in. If you look around, you'll find that the most successful people are the people who learn to adapt to change the fastest. They may not always like or appreciate the change, but they look for the positive in it, or the way it will best suit them, and they begin to work toward their goal in the new set of rules or the changed environment.

Bruce Lee was once quoted as saying, "Empty your mind, be formless, shapeless—like water. Now you put water in a cup, it becomes the cup; you put water into a bottle, it becomes the bottle; you put it in a teapot, it becomes the teapot. Now water can flow or it can crash. Be water, my friend." For a long time, I really didn't understand exactly what he was trying to say, but now it's obvious to me. He was talking about being flexible enough to change in any environment and under any circumstances, and to make the most of change when you do encounter any new situation.

See, the water, in its core composition, is still the same; it will always be $H_2O$. But it has the flexibility to fill any environment it is put in to. We as humans will always be made of the same elements, but can we be like the water—can we be flexible enough to change and adapt to a given situation? It's really quite a unique comparison when you break it down, especially because we as humans absolutely need water to survive and are composed of mostly water. However, if we take in too much water, it can kill us.

Fortunately, change can't kill us. It will feel at times like it is trying to kill us. I promise it will feel that way to a lot of us out there, including myself. At one point, I would resist change so much that I almost lost everything. I didn't know what I didn't know, and I wasn't willing to admit it. See, change requires you to be open-minded and look for opportunities as they come. I thought I was open-minded, but when I took a good long look at what I was doing and the decisions that I kept making, I saw that I wasn't willing to adapt to new circumstances. I was just repeating the same bad decisions over and over again. I would hold on to my old ideas and thought patterns, and I was missing opportunity after opportunity.

My very good friend Maurice Davis used to say, "The problem with holding on to anything too tightly is that no one can give you anything either." He was right. Place a thing in your hands and close them around it as tightly as you can. You'll quickly find that you cannot receive anything else unless you let go of what you're holding on to. For some of us, it's fear; for some of us, it's stubbornness; and some of us are so close to the trees that we can't see the forest. Les Brown has a great quote about how we get blinded by things. He said, "You can't see the picture when you're in the frame."

Oh, there is a bad part to all of this. I might as well warn you now before you go off thinking that change will be completely positive. When you change your mind and it starts to open up, you start to think differently, and you can never go back to the person you were. It's a very strange phenomenon. But for some reason, your mind will remember what you used to do and how you used to think, but now it will only compare your old thought pattern as a bad example to keep you away from making those mistakes again. The biggest downside of change is that the pain you will feel if you try to go back is so amplified that you'll never want to go back. The mind apparently works like a muscle; once it is stretched and grows, it cannot go back to the way it was. Trust me when I tell you there will be a period you will go through where you won't be able to believe that you couldn't, or didn't, see how destructive this old thought pattern was before. It's almost like being given a new set of eyes, and now nothing looks the same through them, and only in a good way.

Don't expect people to see things in the new way you see them. Just because you have opened your mind, do not expect that your family or friends will open theirs. When you start to see the opportunities all around you. Or you begin to point out all the positive things that happen, that before could be seen to be negative. You will spend quite a bit of time trying to convince family and friends that you're not crazy and in fact you do not need therapy. You will have to keep in mind that they are not going to see things the new way you see things. Their minds have been trained to see things in the old patterns that you have let go of. Sometimes you're going to doubt yourself and wonder what happened. You'll think that maybe everyone is right and you're wrong, because they will tell you you're wrong. To use an old analogy, it's the mentality of seeing the glass as either half full or half empty. Others won't understand how in the world do you see the glass is always full no matter what's in it or not in it. Even if it is holding water in half of it, the rest of it is full of air! So therefore the glass is always full!

You will find that as you change your thinking, you will have to change some other things. To become the person you're meant to be, you're going to have to let some things go and some people too. There will be things in your life that you used to do, or used to like, that just won't fit with the person you're becoming. So first I would say: don't get too caught up in material possessions. When you leave this world you can't take them with you anyway. You will eventually find that even though you may want something, you don't need it. It won't be easy, but you'll understand when you start to see the change take place. You'll look at something that you have and think, *Why did I ever find this appealing?* But here comes the harder part: letting go of some of the people who are in your life. It's been said that people come into our lives for a reason, for a season, and for a lifetime. Keep this thought in your mind as you struggle with this. Yes, I said "struggle," because it will be hard to let go of people you love and care about. What you have to understand is that some of the people will become so negative to you that you won't be able to be around them. You won't be able to take all the people with you because some will just refuse to see it like you do. You will have to accept that they don't see the world from the same perspective that you now do and move on with your journey.

It's unfortunate that you will have to go through that, but keep this in mind as well: there will be some people who want to go with you. There will be some who step forward and identify themselves to you, while telling you how they thought they were the crazy ones who thought differently. They'll feel better about knowing that they are not alone, and so will you. I promise this will happen to you, because not everyone is going to agree with you. They won't understand how you used to be this way, or you used to be that way. All you have to say is, "Hey, used to bees don't make no honey," and move on. You have to understand that you can't take your old self into a bright new future; it just doesn't work that way. In order to do something that you've never done before, you've got to be someone you've never been. Einstein said, "The thinking that has gotten me this far has created some problems that cannot be solved by the same level of thinking." He understood that you have to change your thinking to continue to expand, grow, and solve problems in your life.

I heard a person say once that when you look around at the people you hang out with, if you were to find out what wage they made and take the average, you could accurately predict how much money you make. You won't find people who make $1.2 million a year spending too much time with people who make $35,000 a year—not because one group is better than another, but because they think differently. What you'll find is that people are either pouring into you or they are taking from you. So when the time comes and you look around your group and you find you're the smartest one in your group, it's time to get a new group. Again, this is not because you're better or arrogant, but because they group has given you all its members can give, and it's time for you to move on to a new group that has different information and a different way of thinking on a new level.

In everything that you'll face in life, you will have to make a conscious decision to say to yourself, "I can handle this." Think about all the problems you have faced in your life. How hard were they to face, really? Now think about what you know now that you have faced those problems and come through to the other side of them. Did you handle them? Of course you did. There hasn't been anything in your life that you could not handle. I understand that some things you knew were coming, some things you suspected were coming, and some things caught you on the blind side. However, when you look back over a difficult situation or some obstacle that you had to overcome, you have to honestly say that you handled it, or else it would still be a burden in your life. If it is still a burden, then stare it down, decide on a course of action, and handle it.

# CHAPTER 7

## TIME BANDITS

Time lost cannot be regained.

HONESTLY, WE SHOULD probably spend a lot of time here in this chapter.

I know you may be thinking, "Why? I know how to tell time."

But do you? Because the truth is, we really don't "tell" time anything. The fact is that *it* tells *us*. Can you tell me when you will have your first child? When you will get your dream job? When you will find you soul mate? When you will find your passion? When you will live your dream? My guess is that you're starting to get my point: that you don't know, and can't possibly know, when these things will happen. But they all have something in common—time. They will all take place and all occur in time, and most of the time not when you decide they will. I once read a quote that said, "Time: the silent dictator." It's true.

At some point in our lives, we began to think of time as something we control, most likely because humans have a basic need for control. Because we cannot touch time or feel time, we simply decide in our minds that we have control over it. We can schedule our days, our appointments, our haircuts, when we work, what time we pick the kids up—all on our own little schedule that we set on a daily basis. Unfortunately, I have some bad news: we don't control time. The fact is, it controls us, it always has, and it always will. Time can make you old, gray, rich, happy, or sad, and it goes on and on, and all in due time.

One thing you need to understand is that time is not your friend. It does not sit on a shelf somewhere and wait for you to use it. Time only takes from you; it does not give you anything. You give you things by using time, like volunteering your time or helping a friend in need. By doing these types of things, you have set yourself up for some good things to come back to you. You know the old saying, "You reap what you sow"? Well, if you're out there sowing some good things for yourself, what do you think will come back to you? I promise, it works with the positive aspects as well as it works with the negative aspects. Unfortunately, we tend to only ever look at the negative side. Time itself has no plans for you, other than the one promise it does have for you—that eventually your time will expire. As humans, we are a funny breed. We like to think that somehow we control time and we can pull it out and use it whenever we want. How many times have you thought about doing something and said, "I'll get to it when I have more time"? When you *have more time*? Where are you going to go to get this time? There is no store that I know of where you can buy more of it. And one of the most unique characteristics of human beings is our innate way of figuring out how to waste things.

Think of some examples of all the ways we have figured out to waste things—food, water, and even money. In fact, we are so good at wasting things, we have even figured out how to waste some things in advance. Take, for example, the credit card. This is the biggest waste of money in advance. Most of the time, we use credit cards to satisfy some greed we have now, and we promise to pay later when we get the money. By that standard, we are actually wasting our money in advance of even getting it. The worst part is that, by the time you actually pay the bill, there's a pretty good chance you don't even like that shirt you bought any more. You probably don't care about that game anymore, or don't even have the item. Yet you wasted money in advance for it, and paid interest to waste that money. Doesn't sound very smart, does it? But for some reason, we as humans excel at it. We do it and convince others that it's a good idea.

It's strange that we are all given twenty-four hours each day when we wake up, and in those twenty-four hours, we get to choose how we spend each minute. Can you imagine if there was a penalty for wasting time? What if you wasted an hour watching some rerun on TV on Monday, and then, when you opened your eyes on Tuesday, you found out the penalty for the wasted time was that you only got twenty-three hours on Tuesday? I know it's impossible, but there are a whole bunch of us who are guilty of wasting time. Can you imagine how much trouble we would be in if we could figure out how to waste time in advance like we waste money?

Thank God we haven't figured that out, and most likely will never be able to. We have attempted to do it through procrastination, though. The problem is that you can't waste time in advance because it's not there; it doesn't exist yet. It absolutely does not show up until the next minute, hour, or breath. The downside is that it's gone as fast as it came. Show me on a calendar the day called "tomorrow." I've got a hunch it doesn't exist there, and never has and never will. Why? Because in reality there is no tomorrow, there is only right now, this minute! After the minute passes, it existed, but will never exist again. We only know it was there because we lived it. However, we don't know that the next minute is there. Yet we trick ourselves into believing it is always there, or clocks wouldn't have minutes on them, right?

So why am I talking about this and trying to drive home this point about time? I think it is important to understand that the only guarantee that time has for you is that you don't make it out of here alive. To put it another way, you have to die to leave this life. So when we talk about time, it's important to have a firm concept of how it works, so that you can clearly identify the "time bandits" when you see them.

Time bandits will come in and out of your life in all different shapes and sizes. For some people, they show up as video games; for others, they show up as friends; and for still others, they will be television. But you'll know them by the amount of time you spend doing them and by the fact that you have no feeling of accomplishment afterward. I'm not saying to never take a break; of course you'll have to take a break, but make sure you only allow a set amount of your time to be wasted in doing so. I tell you to compare it to your eating plan: I love sugar. But I also know now that if I consume too much sugar, I will gain weight. I also love coffee, of course with sugar in it. So I created a spot in my life to have this mixture, and it's only on Saturday morning. It's my time to have my coffee with sugar, just the way I like it, but I do it in a manner that will keep the pounds off!

I know some people will say, "Well, it just isn't that easy." They are wrong; it *is* just that easy. All it boils down to is making a decision. You're not being asked to rob a bank, kidnap a child, or commit some other crime. We're talking about you taking control of your time. You have to understand that if you don't control your time, someone or something else will. Unfortunately, when this happens, you will not always like the end result. So if you don't control how your time is spent, you'll look around, and the next thing you know, a year has gone by, then five years, and then ten years, and you'll wonder where the time went.

See, it's not in our power to control that time is going to happen; none of us has the ability to make the clock stop. What is within our control is how we manage the time we have and what we do with it. That is why I say it's as easy as making the decision to start changing how you spend your time. I challenge you: if you take action and take the necessary steps to change the way you spend your time, things will start to fall into place. Obstacles that you were facing or decisions that seemed difficult to you, that just seemed insurmountable, will become easier and easier. You'll find avenues and paths that will open up for you that you didn't realize were there. People will come into your life to help you. It is a very amazing thing when you go into action, and help that you didn't even know was possible gets sent your way. So please understand that the time is now!

# CHAPTER 8

# FEAR AND COURAGE

End only means Effort Never Dies.

I REMEMBER I was reading an interview one time. It was with NBA legend Michael Jordan. The interviewer asked him how much fear he felt every time he was asked to take a last-second, game-winning shot. His reply was remarkable. Mr. Jordan said to the interviewer, "None."

In disbelief, the interviewer pushed for more. "None? Oh, come on, with all the pressure and a lot of the time in play-off games or in the finals?"

Michael Jordan retorted, "It would be ridiculous of me to worry about or be afraid of a shot I haven't taken yet. I don't know the outcome, so why worry about it?" After reading that, I thought Gatorade should have changed its ads from "Be like Mike" to "Think like Mike."

A lot of us get trapped there, in the fear of the unknown, and our minds lead us to doubt ourselves. If we had to do challenge ourselves to handle a situation or make a tough decision, could we handle it? Stop for a moment and think about the absolute worst day of your life. I want you to really experience it again. What was going on? What season was it? What did the air smell like? Who was there? Once you have that image planted firmly in your mind, I want you to think about the total outcome. What happened to you? I have to believe that you didn't die, so how bad was it really? Was there some pain? I'm sure there was; life is pain. You are going to go through some pain. You can't hide from it, because it will come find you. I heard a man say once, "Pain and struggle is the rent you pay for being allowed to take up a space on this planet."

I think a lot of times we try to cut a deal with life, and the fact is, there's no deal. Life does not make deals with anyone. I hear people say all the time, "Why did this happen to me?" They usually don't like it when I say, "Because it was supposed to." The powers that be decided you were the one who could handle it. People spend too much of their time being afraid and trying to be good so life will be good back to them. It's a myth that if you never let yourself feel too good, then you'll never get hurt too badly. I'm sorry to inform you that you're going to get hurt, and you're going to be afraid at times. I like what Zig Ziglar says about fear, that it is an acronym that stands for "false evidence appearing real."

I'm not saying that you should never feel fear or experience it. I think you should, or otherwise you can't grow. I say this because if you're not feeling fear and feeling uncomfortable, that means you're still inside your comfort zone, and the problem is that nothing grows there. What I am suggesting to you is that fear is a state of mind. It's a pattern of thought, and just like with all patterns of thought or states of mind, it can be changed. Some people don't realize how powerful their mind is. Trust me when I say that your mind *can* overcome your fear.

Fear is actually a prediction that we make about the way something may or may not turn out. We actually end up tricking ourselves into being afraid of a possible outcome that has not happened yet. We tend to let that fear get a hold of us and paralyze us as if there is nothing we can do about it. The fact is, all you have to do is keep pursuing your dreams. Time is going to pass whether or not you take action. The difference is that if you face your fears, you'll find that Franklin D. Roosevelt was correct when he famously said, "The only thing we have to fear is fear itself." What did he mean by that? I now take it to mean that the thing you should be most afraid of is that fear will try to stop you from accomplishing everything and anything that you want to do. Roosevelt also said "Happiness lies in the joy of achievement and the thrill of creative effort."

Let's look at it in another light. Some people take a worst-case look at things: if you decide to do something, what's the worst that can happen? You may fail, people may laugh, they may try to talk you out of it, you may not have enough money at the time to accomplish your goal, you may not have access to resources, and people may start to not like you. Quite honestly, all this is OK. If someone doesn't support and encourage you to become what you came here to be, then do you really need that person in your life? Sometimes you have to check the fruit on the tree. You judge a tree by the fruit that it bears. So do a "fruit check." If you thought you had an orange tree, and you bite into the fruit only to find out it was a grapefruit tree, not only are you going to be a little dazed and confused by what just happened, but you probably would also decide to cut the grapefruit tree down because it's not what you wanted; or you may get some sugar to put on top of the grapefruit and decide to eat that darn thing anyhow. After all, you already invested the time in cultivating the tree, didn't you? So when unexpected events happen to you, do an assessment of how important that thing or person is in your life. Don't waste your time on people who only want to hold you down.

Take, for example, my friend Jason Johnson. Here's a man who could tell you all about fear. Here's a man who has served his country admirably, and continues to serve even as I write this. He continues to pursue his passion of training K-9 units for the military and for private use, to find explosives. He teaches young men and women how to properly use a trained K-9 and the relationship they need to have with the animal. If you ever meet him, just ask, and he'll tell you. It's his passion, working with these magnificent animals and people who in turn help keep us safe and let us enjoy a worry-free life. Yet despite the example of some dedicated individuals like Jason, we have the audacity to not pursue our dreams and passion in the face of fear. Somehow we think it's OK for us to chicken out.

People say, "But Jason was in the military, so he understands that he has to have courage in times of fear." I will tell you what I have learned about courage. Make no mistake; courage is certainly not the absence of fear. If you talk to enough people, in particular men and women who have been in or are currently in the military, what you'll find is that, in almost every case, they feel fear. Courage is actually feeling the fear but doing whatever is causing the fear anyway. You have to understand that sometimes there is no retreat. Sometimes you will feel afraid, but courage comes in when you feel the fear, accept it, and start working on the task anyway.

Speaking of dogs, I am reminded of a story of a young man who, on his walks home from school, would get to a certain block. As soon as he walked past a certain house, this mean, snarling dog would come racing off the porch and chase him down the street, just barking and barking at the young man. So he would take off running, all the while the dog was in hot pursuit. This continued for several weeks, until finally the young man decided he had had enough. Just up the street was a construction site, and he thought he would lead the dog there, and then he could grab a board or something and go to battle with this dog. So the next day, as he walked past the house, that dog came off the porch toward him as usual. The young man ran as fast as he could with the dog in hot pursuit, snarling and barking. The boy made it to the construction site, grabbed a brick, and turned around quickly to throw it at the dog. As the dog raced up, the boy cocked his arm, but he caught a second glimpse of the dog as it approached. It was then that he noticed that the dog didn't have any teeth in its mouth and could have never done him any harm anyway. The young man snapped at the dog, "Go home!" The animal tucked its tail between its legs and trotted off back home. I tell you this story because this is what most of us do. We are petrified, and we spend all our time running away from things that don't have any teeth and couldn't hurt us anyway. The fear we think we feel is simply all in our mind.

You're probably saying, "No, no, no, it can't be that simple, that it's just in my mind."

The fact is that it really is all in your mind. It's a trick that you have actually played on yourself.

You're now saying, "Yeah, but my heart starts racing, and my palms get sweaty, so how can it be in my mind when I see the physical reaction?"

Yes, you see a physical reaction because it's the body's natural reaction when your mind feels fear. The body doesn't care if the fear is real or false. It produces the same reaction to what it perceives as fear, even if the fear is false fear.

My uncle Peter Gach served in the military during World War II. He was there when the Allied forces stormed the beaches of Normandy. You'll never get me to believe that as a young man he wasn't afraid of what was going to happen when they arrived at that beach. According to him, all the soldiers knew what they were headed for. And these men sat on those boats, riding along, just waiting for the doors to drop so they could try to make a run for the beach. I can tell you, because I've looked in his eyes as he told me the story of that day, that he was afraid, but he did it anyway. He knew there was a higher purpose, and at the time he wanted to return to his passion: my aunt Honey. But he would tell you that after going through this experience, any time he was faced with any future difficulty, he would think to himself, *I made it through that, so this here is nothing.*

My uncle went on to become very wealthy by pursuing his passion with plastics. He had a vision that society was headed that way and ended up inventing the safety tab on plastic containers. You know, that little ring of plastic that is on almost every bottle you open now days. He also invented the push-down-and-turn safety cap that you find on almost every medicine bottle. The funny part is that he invented these things because he didn't want his children to be at risk of getting into something that could harm them. He also had a very successful gas station and a nursery, because he loved working with plants. He wasn't looking to be rich; that was just a by-product of his actions. If you ever travel to Evansville, Indiana, you will now know why there is a street called Gach Drive.

# CHAPTER 9

# THE COMFORT ZONE

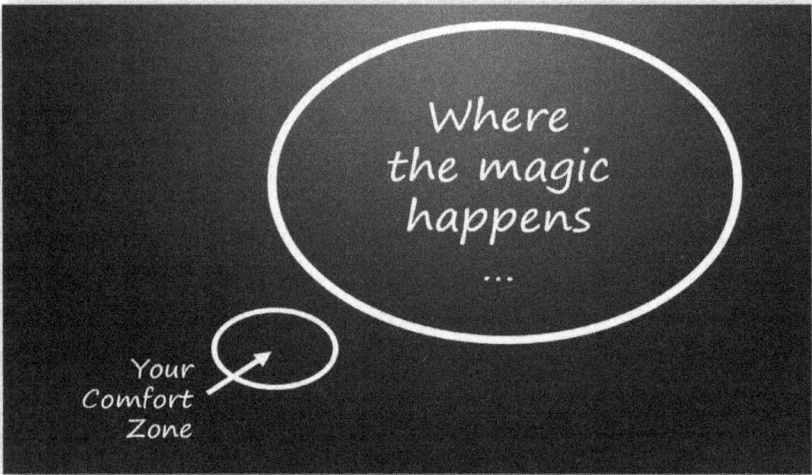

When you see there's nothing left to learn in
your area, it's time to find a new area.

AH, THE COMFORT zone; yes, it's that magical place where nothing happens. That really cool place where fear keeps us from being more than what we are. But we like to feel comfortable, like we are the kings of our domain. It's nice, pleasant, and warm there. You know that place—the one where you have control and you know all the answers.

The funny thing about that place is that it doesn't really exist. It's another one of those things that's all in your mind. The truth about the comfort zone is that nothing grows there; in fact, it will actually suck the life out of you. Society seems to struggle with the idea that the only time you are truly growing is when you feel uncomfortable. The sad truth of the whole thing is that if you would just take a small step outside that zone, you would honestly be amazed at how much is there waiting for you.

How many times in your life have you said to yourself, "If I had known it was that easy, I would have done that a long time ago"? I would guess that I've probably said this at least a dozen or more times in the last week—so there's no telling how often I've thought so over my whole life. You'll find more often than not that all of the magic happens just outside the comfort zone. Most people will start on a project or a journey, and the minute they start to feel uncomfortable, they quit. If they would have just gone one or two more steps to get outside of their comfort zone, they would have had whatever they wanted.

But it's hard to take that step into the unknown. We always want to have some assurance that we will be great the first time we try anything out. The problem is that there is no proof that you'll be great the first time out. What there is proof of, and what you can take to the bank, is the fact that if you don't try, you'll never know what would have happened, and you'll definitely fail.

Now, some people will stop right there and say, "Well, see, that way I can't be disappointed," and that's true. If you don't start, you'll only have to deal with regret, but you're right, you won't be disappointed.

But let me ask you: can you honestly tell me that you have never been disappointed in life? Even when you made the decision to not make a decision, can you honestly look over where you are in life and say you have never been disappointed once? We both know the answer to that. The fact is, if you had climbed into the ring and got in the fight, you would have had so much less disappointment to contend with in the arena of life. What you don't have is the right to stand to the side and tell people how hard it is when you never stepped in the ring to take a punch.

You see, when you get in control and start making the little decisions to get outside your comfort zone, you begin to look at things differently. What I mean by this is that you will get to a point where you will no longer internalize failures or disappointments. You will look at whatever the outcome is with a mind-set that "hey, it just wasn't meant to be," or "it's too bad this doesn't work that way; I'll have to find another way." Your mind will automatically start to function in a way that will help solve problems or will get you past obstacles in your life. Understand that your mind is a problem-solving machine. It doesn't know how to do anything else. It's like if your blood starts getting depleted of oxygen: in such a case, your mind solves the problem by making you breathe faster and heavier to take in more oxygen. From basic needs to the most complicated tasks, your mind will figure things out. It may not always happen as fast as you would like, but it will happen.

I remember taking a math exam while I was in college. It was in algebra, which I wasn't terrible at, but I wasn't the fastest mathematician in the world either. Now, part of my prior work experience was in construction; I had worked with my hands to build things. I don't remember the actual problem as it was written, but I remember the basics of the problem. The instructor had drawn an inground pool, and the homeowner wanted a three-foot walkway all the way around the pool. What the instructor wanted to know was how much cement would be required in square feet. He gave us the equation, and I honestly tried to work through it the best I could. Of course, it was a "show your work" type of problem. It was also a bonus question, and I knew that I had struggled with a couple other problems, so I wanted the extra points. I could only get so far through the equation before I would get stuck; then I'd go some more and get stuck again. Eventually I came to an answer, but something in my mind told me it wasn't correct. As I sat there looking at the drawing, my mind solved the problem. I literally began to see the pool as four separate parts: top, bottom, left, and right. Once my mind split it up, I was able to work the square footage of what was now four sides, and then all I had to do was total it up. Now, I knew the answer I got from using the second method was correct because I had figured these types of things out before when I was working on construction projects, so I submitted it as my answer. The funny part about all of this was that I was correct, but the teacher was trying to follow the work and could not figure out how I had come to the correct answer. Later that week, he asked me to stay after class to show him how I had solved the problem. Ultimately, he was impressed, but he explained to me that was not really what he was looking for. However, he gave me the extra points based solely on the fact he was impressed that no matter what, I had figured it out.

The mind is a very powerful tool, but we just don't apply it to anything. We simply let it sit there and rot away. If we would just push it outside of our comfort zone a little bit, it would not only give us ideas, but it would show us solutions. The fact is that you have to force it outside of the comfort zone. It won't go by itself. It needs to have direction, and guess who the director is, that's right, it's you. You're the one. You came to here to do something and accomplish something that's bigger than just being satisfied with mediocrity, so put your mind to work. Remember how in chapter 5, we discussed how lazy the mind will be if we let it? All you have to do is put your mind to work, and it will automatically get busy figuring out the problem.

People say silly things all the time; they give all kinds of excuses as to why they can't or shouldn't do something. I now have problems understanding why people don't look at the flip side of the coin. You know it's there because it has to be there. Because when you're standing at the edge of your comfort zone looking at what you want to do, it's OK to look at the why nots, but make sure you flip the coin over and look at the other side too. All the reasons why you should do it, and all the things that could go right. These positive possibilities include how much better your life and the lives of your family members will be, how much joy and happiness your decision could bring to your life and the lives of others around you, and how much it could help your community or society. It's funny that people never focus on those things; they only focus on the problems. The fact is, there are no problems, only solutions. William Shakespeare's character Hamlet said, "There is nothing either good or bad, but thinking makes it so."

The best way to get out of your comfort zone is to start spending a lot more time *doing* and a lot less time thinking of reasons not to do anything. All you really have to do is start small. Just think of some little, small thing that has been bothering you, and change it just a little bit. Just push outside your comfort zone just an inch, and I'm sure you'll find it can only benefit you.

For example, I have a friend whose wife always overspent at the grocery store. I suggested to him one day that he make up a budget for the store and only give his wife that much money in cash, so that no credit or debit cards could be used. See, it usually hurts worse when you're spending cash and not swiping plastic; you tend to make better decisions when you can actually see the money you're spending. One of the reasons I suggested this to him was that he had told me about all the food they had been throwing away on a weekly basis. I told him his wife would not be happy, but if he tried just giving her cash, he'd see that she could work within the budget.

Needless to say, he finally got fed up and decided to put my suggestion to the test. Now, this was way outside his comfort zone because he did not like confrontation. When his wife found out, she was furious and exclaimed they would not have enough food for the week. The ironic part of this was that they actually had two refrigerators and a freezer full of food already. So the first week came and went, and he really heard nothing about the change. So he kept up with the budget, the second week went by, and still nothing. Three months later, his fuel pump went out on his truck that he used to get to work, and because of the budget he had put into place, they had the money to pay for the repair and towing in cash, and they still had some cash left. So then he restricted the budget even more, and his wife showed the same anger, but no one in his family was starving, and in fact, his kids were asking that some things just not be bought anymore. So here's the big eye-opener: his family went from spending anywhere from $600 to $800 a week on groceries to only about $300 a week, and there's still plenty of food around the house, but now his family is not throwing anywhere near as much in the garbage.

So get out of your comfort zone. Like my friend in the example above, just try little things and see what kind of effect they have on your life. Go ahead and start writing that song that's been in your head. Go take a class in martial arts that has always interested you. Go to a museum and look around; see if anything strikes your fancy. Go try a wine tasting, even if you have never been interested in doing so before. If you would just go out and try things that make you feel uncomfortable, you'd find that they are not so bad. You see, to be the person you have never been, you have to do some things that you have never done previously. Likewise, to do some things you've never done before, you've got to be a person you've never been. It's the only way that you'll ever be able to grow and become the person that you want to be and, more importantly, to become the person you were meant to be.

# CHAPTER 10

# CALCULATED LEAPS

Sometimes you need to leap and grow your wings on the way down.

WHAT IS A calculated leap? For that matter, what is a leap, and how do we calculate it? The first thing that we need to understand in taking a leap toward anything is that we have to be willing to be flexible with what the various outcomes may be. Once you take a leap, no matter how much planning you have done, I can assure it will almost never fall into place the way you thought it would happen. Now, that does not mean that you can't get the outcome you want. It may just be a matter of decisions you will have to make and small corrections that will have to take place to reach the outcome you want.

Let's look at some examples of calculated leaps and what the outcomes are. For example, have you ever seen a long jumper prepare for a distance leap? If you notice, these athletes stand back and stare at the mark they want to hit. They visualize it in their mind; they see their feet landing exactly on the spot they want to reach. In their mind's eye, they begin to calculate how fast they need to be running, how much muscle force will be required when they jump, and how far their momentum can carry them before they reach the target. Once they think they have it figured out, they line up and wait for the gun or buzzer to sound, and they take off for the line, running faster and faster, breathing heavier and heavier. The closer they get to the takeoff line, the more they start to concentrate on the liftoff, and then, *bam!*—they lift off. If you watch them in the air, you would swear they are double-jointed. The flexibility they have while sailing through the air is unbelievable. Their arms extend way back behind them, as do their legs. Their spine appears to actually be deformed, as you've never seen anyone's curve that far before. In a single movement, both the jumpers' arms and legs come forward again, giving them just a little more momentum, before they touch back down on the ground, having hit their target. This is just a brief description of what this looks like. Now, I'll tell you what you don't see. You don't see them show up just before it's their turn to jump and walk to the line, staying as rigid as possible, like a four-by-four post; wait for the gun to sound; and then hop forward. No, they use every muscle, every bit of concentration, and focus on their goal.

To give you another example, let's look at the calculated leap of going from the earth to the moon. First, we have to realize that the two celestial bodies are not always in alignment with each other, so there have to be some serious calculations in taking spacecraft from the earth to the moon. For hours and days, sometimes months and years, before the mission-control team members begin to ready a crew for the shuttle, they have to look at weather patterns, planet alignment, and any floating debris; also, today they have to consider where the satellites are, where the space station is, and if any other country has sent up a rocket or shuttle. All of these things have to be looked at and taken into consideration before they can launch anything. Sometimes even after all these things are considered, mission control ends up scrubbing the launch anyway because of some other unforeseen problem. Now, it's my understanding that when the rocket took off from Earth, during the entire trip to the moon, the spacecraft was only on course for a few hours. The rest of that time, the onboard computer and mission control was recalculating the trajectory and correcting the path of the rocket to ensure it arrived at its destination. Could you imagine if mission control just aimed a rocket toward the moon one night, and launched it? Do you think that would be all that was required to make it to the moon? Of course not; little corrections have to be made because everything is changing. It's all in constant motion, and without making those corrections and taking all factors into consideration, the astronauts would not make it to their destination. Believe me when I tell you that they certainly do not fly in a straight line. I can tell you even from my training as a pilot that once you have plotted your course and you take flight, you never know what will happen. The wind could change from a headwind to a crosswind and begin to blow you off course. Again, you will have to make corrections. Even as you cross isogonic lines, you will have to make magnetic corrections. There's a lot that goes into making it from point A to point B, and your path is almost never in a straight line unless you make the necessary corrections.

I imagine that most of you reading this have either driven or ridden in a car at some point. OK, now imagine someplace you would like to go to. Pick out all the places you would like to stop along the way toward that destination. Now you have that image good and planted in your mind. Great, now let's get in the car; what the heck, you go ahead and drive, and I'll be the passenger. But once you start the car, here's the catch: I want you to put your hands on the wheel at ten and two like you're supposed to. OK, now you've got that, great; now just drive straight forward without ever turning the steering wheel. How far did you make it? What, not very far? You're kidding me. You mean even to do something as simple as driving a car, you have to make turns and corrections? I couldn't even get out of my driveway if I tried to just drive in a straight line. I have to make little corrections to turn out into the street. You and I both know the example I've just given is a little ridiculous, but it still makes the same point: you can't drive down a lane on a highway without making little adjustments or corrections. If you've ever tried this, you've find quickly that you are changing lanes or running onto the shoulder of the road.

Do you remember when you first started driving? Remember how nervous you felt, how much pressure was on you? Especially if Mom or Dad was in the passenger seat next to you. That's right, you kept both hands on the wheel and made sure you always signaled and checked all your mirrors before changing lanes. What you didn't know at the time was you were taking a calculated leap. You knew that others could do it, and you had been told how you're supposed to do it, so this gave you confidence that driving was a risk worth taking.

It was really nothing more than a calculated leap of faith that others could do it, and so you felt determined to figure out how to do it as well. You wanted to be able to drive from point A to point B, rather than ride a bike or walk. Can you imagine if you had talked yourself out of it before you even got started? I imagine the conversation would have to include people who had tried driving and didn't like it—and also the people who could give you all the statistics about how many people die in car accidents each year, or the people who talk themselves into believing that cars are only for the wealthy. Let's face, it the majority of us couldn't afford a car when we first started driving, so we either had to get a loan or buy a cheaper car that may have needed some repairing (and we didn't know how to repair a car either). So even that was a further calculated leap: that we would get a good car that would not break down and cost us more money that we didn't have.

So what did you do when buying your first car? You weighed the odds and decided that you wanted to be able to drive and move around quicker than other forms of transportation would allow. You took a calculated leap to attempt something you had never done before, that you had never owned before, that you had never repaired before. Yet here you are still alive, and doing great! So why is one calculated leap so much easier than another is? The only possible answer is that it's all in your mind's eye. Do you want it badly enough to do the work and to learn about the outcomes? How much are you willing to do? Your dream will always come back to you, and you will need to be willing to look over the given information and make a commitment about what you want to do.

Here's what I can tell you about taking the calculated leap. I'll give you this one statistic, because it's truly the only one needed if you're wondering how many people take a calculated leap and make something out of it. That's easy to answer: it's one hundred percent. That's it, that's the big number. I'll say it again, it's one hundred percent of the people who decide. The fact is that if you look at what it is you want to do, take in all the factors around you, formulate a commitment, set goals, and work diligently to achieve those goals, then you make it. There is no other possible outcome. So the real question is this: have you decided?

Have you decided that whatever it is that you want; that you think about all the time; that makes it hard to fall asleep at night, and when you do fall asleep, you find it there in your dreams as well—have you decided that this dream is important enough to you that you have to go do it? That your life will seem useless and pointless without it? That you're willing to work for it, and be told no and have people laugh at you, and disrespect you, and tell you how dumb that sounds and how you can't do it? Are you willing to take the criticism and the finger-pointing and the sideways glances and the days of solitude?

Are you willing to keep looking yourself in the mirror and reassuring yourself that you are making the right choices, and these are the decisions that you need to be making? Are you willing to give up who you *are* for who you will *become*?

I say to you, never be afraid to let go of the good to grab the great! You see, greatness is caused when there's no applause. That's the big secret; it doesn't happen like you see it in the movies. You won't sit in a theater that long—that is, movies don't last five, ten, or twenty years, or an entire lifetime, to show you what the people who achieved their dream went through. In the same way, your success happens in the quiet of your own mind, when there's no one around. It occurs in all the following cases: when there's no one cheering you on, when you make the decision that you're going to make it, when you sell out to you, when you decided that you're good enough, when you know that you deserve whatever it is you're after—and when you finally decide to stop listening to that chatterbox in your mind that tells you about all the things that could go wrong, and you instead start listening to that little voice that tells you about the possibilities of the things that could go right.

So my suggestion to you is that, when you start to look at what a calculated leap is and if you should take that leap, listen to that voice that tells you about all the things that could go right. If you take the leap and fail, it doesn't mean it was a bad idea. It just means that you have to change your approach to how you are going to achieve that goal. One of the biggest things that you'll have to retrain yourself on is that failure is not bad. I'll say that again: failure is not a bad thing. We are taught to believe it's bad, but in and of itself, it's not. Beware of the man who's never failed, because he never did anything.

# CHAPTER 11

# QUALITY OR QUANTITY?

Quality is not an act, it's a habit.

Wow, NOW HERE'S a tough choice: do you want quality, or do you want quantity? Most of us would say quantity. It's funny that when we human beings look at things, we always think more is better. So if you got stung by one bee, getting stung by one hundred is better! Seriously, though, ask my wife; she will completely argue this with you as she is highly allergic to bee stings. But if you look around, you can see this preference reflected in everything we do, and even more so in everything we buy— you know, the little things, like how a sixteen-ounce jar of mayonnaise is probably good enough, yet we'll buy the ten-pound jar because it's on sale. We never really stop to think about why we are buying it; we just do it. That is what leads us into a lot of our problems: we have a broken way of looking at things that causes us to keep doing instead of thinking. If you really ask yourself how often you eat mayonnaise, you will probably realize it's not often enough to warrant buying the ten-pound jar. Chances are that it will spoil before you use 98 percent of it, and you will have to throw it out.

My grandmother always fell victim to this type of thinking when she would go to the store. If she found a coupon for a dollar off something, she was buying that item. I used to literally have to bring jars of Miracle Whip home and give it away because she didn't like it, and we didn't use it at our house either. But if it was on sale and she had a coupon, she bought it, because she was saving money. See, to me, that is not a quality opportunity. It may be a quantity one, because by the end of it, I finally had to tell her to stop because my friends could not eat it as fast as she was buying it. She was giving away her money on something she didn't need and didn't like. Where's the quality in that? Now, I realize this is an extreme example. Still, it doesn't make it any less true. You have to see how there was no quality involved in that quantity opportunity. You may have a bunch of Miracle Whip, but by the time you go to use it, the quality is not going to be all that great.

When I talk about "quality," I mean what's important to you. That's really where a quality opportunity comes from. You have to look at something—an idea, an opportunity—and make a judgment call on how important it is to you. In this game of life, your opinion of what you want to do and to have for yourself is the only one that really matters, so you will have to make choices and decisions based on you. Don't let anyone else influence you with what he or she thinks is important. It has to be a quality opportunity for you, not your neighbor, or your brother, or Jimmy down the street. It has to matter to *you*. You have to see the benefit in it, the quality it will bring to your life.

I know a guy who is a cancer survivor and a heart-attack survivor, and who has the ability to do whatever he wants with his life. He had to beat this terrible disease of cancer, yet he will not quit smoking. Oh, sure, he stopped for a little while, but then I think that something snuck into his mind—maybe he thinks he's invincible, or maybe he just thinks he can win at anything. While that is a great mind-set to have, the problem is that he tends to lean toward the negative view of life. I think you can see he's not really giving himself a quality opportunity.

The truth is that opportunities come along all the time. The problem is that most of us don't listen. There's that still, small voice in our heads that tells us, "Hey, that looks like a good opportunity," and then we tune out that voice, and we listen to what the world has told us instead: "If it looks too good to be true, it probably is." The negative things that the world has taught us live in our memories, and most of us live out of our memories because doing so is all we know. So we talk ourselves out of so many opportunities that were probably quality opportunities. No, I am not crazy enough to think that all opportunities are quality ones. But most of us will cut off an opportunity before we even begin to investigate it. We don't even get any information. We shut it down in our mind based on the limited information we have and on opinions that we think may or may not be true. The worst part is that some of those opinions are not even ours. They were handed down or given to us by someone else. We accepted them as our reality, and we choose to live with them—but we don't have to.

The fact is that when you look around at opportunities, they usually disguise themselves as work. That's right, I said it—work—and work is hard, and no one wants to do more work than he or she has to, right? Here's the problem with that: if you don't do the extra work, you can't have the extra things. I once heard a person say that you must do the things today that others aren't willing to do so you can have the things tomorrow that others won't have. It's true, and in your heart you know

64

it's true. You don't get overtime pay at work by sitting home, do you? No, of course not; even though the big football game is on Saturday, you accept the overtime or the call to come in, if you want the extra money. The end result is that your paycheck is bigger than that of the guy who refused the overtime, or who saw the caller ID and decided to let it go to voicemail.

Let's take a look at the quantity of opportunities that you see. It would probably surprise you that there's pretty good chance you pass up hundreds of opportunities a week, and probably a day. Are all of them quality opportunities? Probably not; some make only take you so far and drop you. Some might take you in the direction of where you want to go, but then again, some might take you exactly where you need to go. Not all opportunities will always yield the results that you ultimately want. I have had opportunities come my way where I didn't understand what I was looking at, but I thought it was something I should do. More times than not, the opportunity didn't get me to my goal; however, it did put me in touch with a person who could help get me there.

For example, I took a contract once to do work for a certain company. I didn't particularly like the area that the job was in, but I thought it might be a good experience. I quickly found out that I really didn't like the job or the long hours, but I had accepted the contract and planned to see it to the end. During my time working there, the engineering staff began to gain a lot of confidence in my abilities to talk and relate to people. They would send me parts that were for future products and ask me to go to world headquarters to get approval for surface appearance or texturing. Then this process became the norm. I really didn't mind this part of the job so much; I got to meet a lot of interesting people whom I would have never had the chance to meet otherwise. Then, eventually, I was taking the parts to technical engineering labs to have them mapped for texturing. This was how I met Ray.

Ray worked for the company that did the graining for tooling, the graining that you see on most door panels and dashboards in cars and trucks. Ray and I got to know each other really well and had to call each other quite a bit during the busier times of releasing a new product. In fact, if Ray was having problems with an engineer, he would sometimes call me and ask if I could help. I would jokingly tell him to remember the favor for later. But over a period of time, Ray and I got to work together less and less. You see, management had changed at the company I had the contract with, and my hours were cut, and the workload was pushed on to the engineers, whom management thought should have been doing the job all along.

But I never forgot Ray; he was just such an incredible person and always had a smile on his face. He always had the most amazing stories about parts that he had seen or things that were supposed to come out on vehicles that had never made it to production. Then one day it happened. I was talking with some engineers about a part I was redesigning for a company. We had walked through the entire process of manufacturing the parts—from configuring the design, to 3-D printing of a prototype, to getting tooling made and seeing what a final product would look like and cost. Then it came time to have one final step done. You guessed it: I needed to have the tooling mapped and grained. Who do you think came to mind? That's right, my old friend Ray. He and I hadn't talked for some time, so I was a little hesitant about calling him, but I had told the company that was building the tools that I felt Ray would be the best for the job. So I looked for his card and called him up one afternoon.

My heart raced as the phone rang. I got lucky and got his voicemail. Sure enough, it was still Ray's phone. As I was leaving a message, Ray was already returning my call. So I switched lines, and, just like always, there was that friendly voice on the other end. He was so excited to hear from me; he thought the company I had the contract with had let me go, mostly because he had not heard or talked to me about any parts in quite a while. I explained what had happened when management changed, and he said he had met some interesting people since he had worked with me. Ray was quick to point out that he missed working with me, as I always seemed to understand what was needed to get the job done. It was quite a nice compliment. So I hit Ray with my question; I said, "How would you like to help me with a new project?"

Ray exclaimed, "Anything—what do they have you doing?" I explained to Ray that this was a personal project that I had taken on. I gave him all the details that he asked about, and then he asked what company this was for. I told him it was for my company and explained how I had come to work on this and where the part would ultimately end up.

Ray got so excited that I thought he might jump through the phone. He couldn't wait to get started on it. He took the names and numbers of the people who were building the tooling for me and got in touch with them. The people from the engineering company called me that afternoon to find out where I had found this guy. Ray had already called them and gotten as much detail as he could as to when he could map the parts and what type of graining would they need. They told me no one had ever called there so excited and ready to go to work. It was only then that I found out how recommending Ray paid off in other ways. You see, no one was really returning my calls about helping me get my project off the ground until I called this company and spoke with Ed. He got excited immediately and got on board. What I didn't know was that Ed had come to a roadblock and was unhappy with the current company to which he would send tooling for graining, so he personally took my tooling to a meeting with Ray. Well, Ray and Ed hit it off, and now Ed uses Ray to have other tooling and projects textured and grained.

So if we look at the chain of opportunities that transpired here, I think you'll find it's amazing what can happen. I saw an opportunity to make some extra money by taking on a new contract. Then I saw an opportunity to redesign a part, Ed saw an opportunity to do some work and keep his employees working, and Ray saw an opportunity to help an old friend. From that, Ed saw an opportunity to change companies that grain tooling for him, and Ray saw an opportunity to gain another company to employ him and his team for graining work. At the end of the day, from one opportunity it developed into several opportunities that originally I hadn't even imagined. No one could have convinced me that all of this could have happened just as a result of my taking the original opportunity, which was more of a quantity opportunity than a quality opportunity. But I think we can all agree that the quality of the opportunity produced quite a number of both quantity and quality opportunities for people who would not have had them if I had not acted on the initial opportunity.

See, when you don't act or don't do what you know in your heart you should do, everyone loses. It's not just you who misses out; everyone feels the consequences of your actions. They may not know they missed a chance because you didn't act, or they may know they found an opportunity because you did act, but the fact remains the same—that we all lose when you don't act. From my taking action on this one opportunity, how many more opportunities were created for how many people? It's exponential. There's probably no way to even account for just how many, which is the exact reason why you must take action when you see an opportunity. Even one that may seem not so good can turn into something that you never imagined. As Einstein said, "The imagination is the vision of what's to come!"

# CHAPTER 12

# FAITH: TAKE THE LEAP

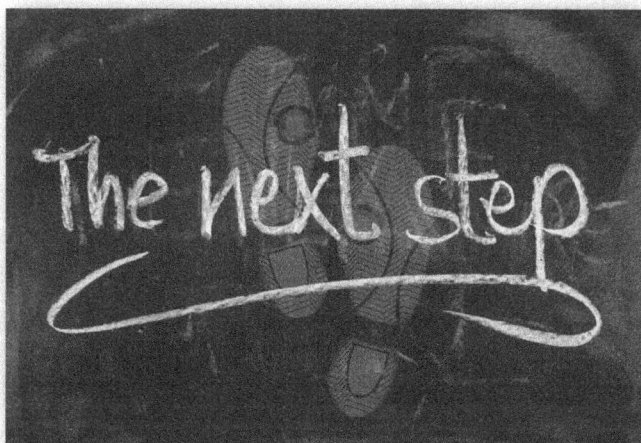

If you don't step forward, you're always in the same place.

FAITH—WELL, WHAT CAN I say; this subject was bound to come up. In fact, it was inevitable that it was going to come up. So what I would like for you to look at or see in a different perspective is the definition of "faith." I am of the opinion that the term can mean more than just faith in God or in a particular religion. Faith is a thing that we touched on a little earlier in the book. Remember in chapter 2 where we talked about learning to walk? See, when you walked for the first time, you had belief, but you also had absolute faith that you could do it. Most of the time people say things like "If I see it, I'll believe it." Unfortunately, with faith, the way it works is that if you believe it, you'll see it.

At some point we tend to lose faith in our own thoughts, and I think we somehow accidentally transfer that loss of faith on to our abilities and ourselves. As we grow up or get disappointed in life, we tend to lose faith that there is really anything we can do about our situation. I am here to tell you that it's not true. You *can* do something about your situation. After you go around beating yourself up mentally, you can correct your thought pattern; the problem is, that change will come through faith. You have to believe and have faith, with everything that you are, that it will happen for you, and it will.

Beginning to look at how we live our lives and how we think about things may help us to understand this idea. Human beings are so unique in that, after we lose faith in ourselves, we begin to live out of our memories. We start acting as if the area of our mind that remembers how things work or fit together is the only way that we can go through life. We act as if our willingness to dream has been beaten out of us by the experience of life. Most of us feel like we have no choice but to live from there because that's all we know. There is a big problem with living from your memory, and that is that the things you remember are not always that good for you. Think about it for a minute; you can tell me everything you did in the last few hours. You can tell me everything you did yesterday, last week, last year, and even over the last several years. So now I ask you to tell me exactly what is going to happen seventeen minutes from now. What's going to happen seventeen hours from now, or seventeen days from now? Then tell me what's going to happen seventeen years from now. You can't, can you? You can't even tell what's going to happen five minutes from now. Why?

The answer is quite simple, really. It's because you haven't lived it yet. There is no memory of what's going to happen. See, you have to go through a time period so that you can then know what happened. I once heard a person say that there are only two days on which nothing can be done: yesterday and tomorrow. He's right; we can't change the past, and we haven't made it to tomorrow to be able to do anything then. So we can only do something right now. So would you imagine that, if you started to make some decisions and choices based on what you would like to see happen, you could help put yourself in the direction of what you would like to see happen tomorrow?

Let's take a look at it this way. Let's say you are washing some clothes that you needed for tomorrow. So you gather them up before you go to bed and take them into the laundry room. The next morning you get up, and there they lie on the floor where you left them. So you get upset and shout, "See, nothing ever works out for me!" Now, what if instead you had gone into the laundry room and put them into the washer with soap and started the machine and then gone to bed? I would guess they would be clean the next morning, but they would be wet too. So what would you have to have done? Well, maybe you would collect the clothes a little earlier than bedtime; run them through a wash cycle; when that's done, throw them in the dryer; and then head to bed. Do you think they would be dry the next morning and ready for you? Of course they should be. Nothing is definite, but you have a better chance of getting to wear clean clothes by following that last example, wouldn't you agree? I mean, there is the chance the dryer could break while you're asleep and they wouldn't be dry, but through your efforts, you did some things can give you a pretty predictable outcome for tomorrow. It's not guaranteed, but you stand a better chance of having the clothes done this way, don't you?

You see, none of us can predict the future with any kind of exact accuracy, but if you put in the effort, you can help to tailor it in the direction you would like to see it go. You have to do some things that you can see some results from, and then your faith will start to return to you. You have to learn to let go of the memories that show you all the bad things that will happen and why you shouldn't count on anything. You see, that's what I am talking about when I say we tend to live out of our memories. Our minds tend to show us all the bad things that come from our memories, and they understand that those things are only things that the world gave us. There is no way you could convince me that you would want any bad things to happen to yourself or to anyone else. Yet we take a mind-set of having no faith, and we believe that only the worst possible outcome is what's possible for us. Why?

Why do we so easily only see the negative things that can happen instead of having faith that if we put some effort in, something really good can happen? How do you think a blind person learns to move around in this world? He or she has faith that if he or she picks that stick up and just starts moving around, that stick will bump into things before the blind person will, and it will serve as a warning to change directions. Have you ever stopped to think that maybe if you pick that stick up and start moving in any direction, that the stick might serve as your warning to change directions? Sure, you may wobble around, and you may stagger. You may even look like you're completely drunk at times and like you shouldn't be walking at all, but remember when you were learning how to walk—you staggered, you stumbled, you looked like you were drunk, but you kept going until you got it. That's what I am asking of you now. Just start moving in the direction that you think you want to go. Yes, you may hit your legs on things. Yes, you may bruise your shin on things, but if you just keep going, you'll get it. I know you will. I have been there. I know how much effort and pain and sweat and tears it will take. But once you get it, no one can ever take it from you. It's yours, and I promise you that whatever it is that you're looking for, it's also looking for you.

You have to learn again to walk by faith and not by sight. We that know the scripture passage that tells us, "Ask, and it shall be given you; seek, and ye shall find; knock, and it shall be opened unto you: For every one that asketh receiveth; and he that seeketh findeth; and to him that knocketh it shall be opened...Whosoever shall say unto this mountain, Be thou removed, and be thou cast into the sea; and shall not doubt in his heart, but shall believe that those things which he saith shall come to pass; he shall have whatsoever he saith" (Matthew 7:7–8; Mark 11:23). Understand that you're not going to go out to the Rocky Mountains and tell one to move and it's going to get out of your way. This is a metaphor: the mountain is your problem, and if you tell the problem to move, it has no choice but to do as you command. Now, understand going into this that these things that you are trying to accomplish will happen. They will not always happen on your timeline, and it will become frustrating, but if you just keep walking and keep moving in the direction that you want your life to go, it will happen. When things don't happen on your timeline, it's really just the universe testing you to see how badly you want it. How long are you willing to keep walking to get what you want? How important is it to you to have it? What kind of resolve do you really have to say, "Come on life, give it up, 'cause I am not going to stop until I get it"?

Eventually life will become tired, and weary of beating on you; eventually it will say, "Let him or her have it. This one's different, this one's not going to stop, until he or she gets what he or she is after." I say leap, and the net will appear.

The problem is not the problem; the problem is your attitude about the problem. If you just have faith that, in your heart of hearts, no matter how bad it is or how bad it gets, you're going to make it, then you are going to make it; the universe does not have a choice. I once heard a guy say, "You're either on your way from a problem, you're in a problem, or you're going toward a problem." It's true; it's called life, and there are going to be little things that happen that annoy us, and we call these little things "problems." Understand that through your faith, you can overcome any problem that comes up. You have the ability to do more and create more than your mind can even conceive. Please do yourself a favor: don't cop out. Don't head to your comfort zone when problems get hard, and say, "Well, I'm doing pretty well; I'm not doing as badly as my neighbor is." What good does that do you to compare yourself to someone you think is doing worse than you in order to try to make yourself feel better? That's nothing more than a cop-out and a time waster.

Never forget that as you go walking down your path, there will be things that get in the way. I agree with Henry David Thorough when he said, "Go where there is no path and leave a trail for others to follow." Don't just do what others do because that is the so-called normal thing. That's a crowded road over there; you don't want to be part of that. Always strive to be on top because it's the bottom that's overcrowded. Yes, it's going to seem weird, and yes, you are going to seem an outcast. Not everyone's going to like you, and you won't be perfect, so just get that out of your head now. You're going to make mistakes; you're going to flop and fail. You're going to doubt yourself, and when you start to doubt yourself, have a team of people around you who cheer you on!

Having positive people around you is especially important because usually you will be surrounded by people telling you how you can't do it. You see, deep inside they want to see you win, because it gives them hope that there is more to life than just working and paying bills. Either way, you need some help, and you need some coaching. No one gets anywhere by himself or herself; even the great Muhammad Ali had his trainer Angelo Dundee. Why? Because you can't see the fight when you're in it. You have to have someone point your weak spots out, or to advise you of different strategies. Someone once said, "We are born individuals, but most of us die copies." You're better than that, and you owe it to yourself to show it to yourself. Always keep your faith in yourself and in God. If your faith ever begins to falter, lean on God's faith in you. Know that He chose you to be here for a reason—find it.

# CHAPTER 13

# LUCK HAS NOTHING TO DO WITH IT

Luck Has Nothing to do With It

Luck is the worst trick the mind can play on you.

THIS LITTLE FAVORITE gem called "luck" is one of the best excuses in the world for why things just don't seem to go our way. It's been said that successful people in the world look around for the circumstances they want, and if they can't find them, they create them. The book of life describes this as "The rain falls on the just and unjust alike." So to break that down, there is no such thing as luck. The opportunities are out there fall on all of us, and they exist for anyone who is actively seeking them.

I find it amusing how many people will use this excuse as the crutch for why they don't get started doing anything. How many times have you heard, "Well, one day my luck will change," or "If I can just get luck on my side"? Has anyone ever seen this luck that everyone seems to talk about? I personally have never seen it. In fact, I have never seen any evidence that it even exists. Yet people will go around sounding off about their bad luck or good luck.

I almost don't even like to hear people wish other people "good luck." I hear it sometimes and think, *You're not serious, are you? You can't possibly believe that luck will save you?* I mentioned earlier in the book if you are looking for something or someone to save you, you need to find a full-length mirror and take a good long look. You're the only superhero in your life. Sure, others will help you, but unless you put yourself into motion, no one will ever even know you need or would like help.

See, none of us does anything by ourselves. We like to cling to this idea that we don't need any help from people, that we are somehow so self-sufficient that there's only us, and we can figure it all out. So let me ask you to think of something that you always wanted to do. It can be anything, even something that you wouldn't have the first clue about how to get started with. OK, you got it. Now, think if you were to get started on it. Would you ask somebody for help, or do you think it would be more plausible to just sit around thinking about it, and maybe luck would send someone in your direction to ask you if you would like to get started on whatever you wanted to do? I'm thinking you would have a much quicker path if you just asked for help, and not just from one person. Ask as many people as you can think of. Nine times out of ten, even if whomever you ask doesn't have the answer, he or she can lead you to someone who does. Or else you can just keep sitting around doing nothing and complaining that you just aren't lucky, when in reality, luck has nothing to do with it.

I heard an interview one time with a baseball player. He was asked about his hitting average. This guy hardly ever missed a ball. No matter what the pitch, he could just about hit them all. The reporter commented to the player, "Hey I saw you in practice, man; you sure can hit the ball well—you're so lucky!"

The player replied, "Yes, the more I show up at practice and the more swings I take and the more balls I hit, the luckier I get."

Think for a moment about any project you ever started. Got it? OK, good. So you had this idea of something you wanted to do, and you got your materials and some information gathered up, and you got started on it. Unfortunately, you couldn't finish it all at one time; it was just too much to do at once. So later on, when you came back to it, had luck come by and finished all up for you, and you saw this, paused, and said, "Oh, wow, look how lucky I am that I don't have to finish this up. Thank you, luck, for dropping by and taking care of all the details and finishing up this little project I was working on"?

I'm guessing if the project got completed, it was you who went back to it time after time, and you were consistent and persistent until the project was finished. My guess is that when you were done, you had a great feeling of accomplishment about what you had created or written. Or, maybe that project is still sitting somewhere unfinished because darn it, luck just hasn't come your way yet and finished it up.

If you're waiting on luck, can I suggest that you stop wasting your time? You see, it's just like the reply the baseball player gave: the more you show up and swing, the luckier you get. The problem is that most people won't even take a swing. They will hide behind luck as the reason why they shouldn't get started doing whatever it is they want to do. How many times have you been guilty of this? How is it that we can manage to let something that in reality doesn't exist stop us from doing something we want to do? The best advice I can give about luck is to let it go out of your mind. It's really just a trick we try to play on ourselves to justify why we're not doing what we know we should be doing. But luck gives us something to hide behind.

I wonder, have you ever thought that maybe, if you just start moving in the direction that you want to go, you would see more things start to happen the way you would like for them to happen? What if, when you got in your car in the morning to go to work, or to run errands or go wherever you needed to go, you just got in, turned the key, and sat there waiting for luck to get you where you needed to go? If it didn't work out and you didn't get anything done, you could just say, "Hey, I guess I wasn't lucky today."

That's how we all get around, right? Of course not. We would never do something like that. Yet still, when you look at that example, you think it's ridiculous, but it's OK to use luck as the excuse to not move in the direction that you want your life to go. Imagine not paying your bills for a month because you might get lucky and someone will pay them for you, or better yet, why not try waiting for luck to come give you a shower in the morning? My guess is that by the week's end, you'd be pretty stinky after waiting on luck to do that for you.

Let me tell you about a time there was a project I had always wanted to do. I had this goal of working for a particular company, mostly due to the product it produced, because I had an idea that I wanted to redesign a piece of it. The more I thought about it, the more I wanted to do something about it. So I asked a franchise owner—we'll call him Dave— what it would take to be involved with the company, and I explained the level to which I wanted to be involved. Dave explained to me how these things would usually work but told me that I would really need to call the headquarters to speak with James, who was the vice president of the company. Dave told me that James was the one who would usually make the decision about whom the company worked with and whom they didn't. Dave explained that if James liked my idea, he might give me limited permission to pursue it and come back to him with some results, and it could be approved.

So at that point I had a name and a number, but it was still up to me to make the call. My biggest fear was that I would get on the phone and get stage fright—you know, like lockjaw or something. Now, the funniest thing about all this was that I knew loosely who James was, and coincidentally, I had spoken to him on the phone once when I had called looking for another employee. I continued to procrastinate and not do anything, but I knew I really wanted to do this, so I would actually call the company and just get used to hearing someone pick up the phone. I would ask some idle question and thank the person and then hang up. Then an idea came to me that if I could come up with more ideas and get James to like one of them, I could get my foot in the door and then try to sell him on the idea that I really wanted to do.

So I came up with three ideas that I thought would be beneficial to the company, and I even had some quick prototypes made up. Now, keep in mind that I had never done any of this before. I actually went and just asked friends if they knew anyone who knew how to do some of the type of things I wanted to do for my ideas. As it turned out, my best friend's fiancée's brother did. The fiancée gave me her brother's number, and we started working on it. I continued to talk to Dave, and then one day Dave said, "What did James say?" and I had to come clean that I had not spoken to James yet. Dave explained that it might be a better plan to talk to James before I invested any more money in my ideas. I had continued calling the office and asking questions unrelated to my project, but finally, one afternoon I waited until right before the close of business, keeping in mind that the company was in a different time zone. I decided that this time I would ask for James. I was pretty sure he would be gone for the day, as it was late on a Friday, but figured I would get used to asking to speak with him.

Guess what…he was there. The receptionist put me right through to him, and now I was stuck. He said, "Hello, this is James." I immediately felt my heart jump into my throat, and for a minute I thought about just hanging up.

I managed to squeak out, "Hi, James." I didn't know what to say; I was not prepared for this, because in my mind, he wasn't supposed to still be at work. I mean, really, what would possess a vice president to still be at his place of employment on a Friday afternoon right before closing time, right? Then I explained to him that I had been speaking with Dave and that Dave had suggested I call him.

James then asked me what it was I wanted to speak with him about. I began to explain in a very cracked voice that I had admired the company for years, and that I had these few ideas I wanted to run by him and see if he would have any interest in working with me or having me work on them. He listened to all three of my ideas, and actually, two of the three caught his attention. One was something I just thought would be neat to do, and the other was—that's right—the redesign of the part. He explained to me that I was not the first to come to him with the redesign idea; apparently there had been a guy several years before whom James had asked to put some ideas together, but James had never heard from the guy again.

We continued our conversation for a few more moments, and James said, "I'll tell you what—I will give you verbal, limited permission to start putting ideas together, but get back to me when you can show me more." It was go time!

Believe me, I didn't even pause a second; I began calling all around to find materials that I thought I would need. I looked for artwork that would fit my idea. I asked everyone I knew if they knew someone who could do the things I needed to get done. I started calling any company in the phone book that had anything to do with plastic molding, and I started stopping at metal shops to see if they could cut the materials I needed cut. I was literally going and talking to almost any company that would listen. It wasn't long until I was given a number for a guy who might be able to do the molding work I needed done for the part. I called him, set up a meeting, and met with him. He was a very nice person and was excited while he listened to what I was trying to do. But when I finished, he explained to me that he didn't think he could produce the part; it was just something that he didn't think his company would go along with.

I was devastated. One of the ideas I just thought would be neat was taking off, while the idea I really wanted to do was grounded. I didn't know where to go from here. I had exhausted every connection that I had attempting to get this project off the ground, and I still hadn't been successful in doing this particular thing. It was new and uncharted territory for me; I didn't know how to handle it. Here I was, with James waiting to hear back, putting his money on the idea that I'd turn out like the previous guy whom he just didn't hear from again. I simply didn't know what to do next, so I decided to keep working on the smaller idea so I could at least keep the doorway of communication open.

I actually began sending James e-mails thanking him for the opportunity; these e-mails would also contain descriptions of designs for the apparel project we had talked about. I would ask his opinion on whether he thought the company would have a preference on what style they would like to see. Now, all while I was doing this, I was still trying to figure out how to get the redesign off the ground. I think the worst thing that happened was that James never returned an e-mail to me the entire time. There simply was no return communication. On occasion, I would call and ask to speak with him, and usually the receptionist would tell me he was busy or was not in, but I could leave a message. I would always tell this person to just let him know I wanted to say thank-you for the opportunity and that I was looking forward to hearing from him on the design ideas.

I did this once or twice a month for about a year. I guess this was the point at which I should have just thrown in the towel and said, "Oh well, I guess I'm just not lucky at this. Maybe if I get lucky, someone will call me back. Maybe if I get lucky, James will call me back." Of course there were times when I doubted what I was doing, because I had no idea how to do it. It was hard and painful to have to keep looking in the mirror and telling myself it would all work out, that I should just keep moving. Yet everyday it didn't feel like I was getting any closer to closing the door on this. Finally, I decided to do something that was rather unusual. *I was struggling to get back in touch with James, but I knew someone who wouldn't have the same problem.*

I finally called Dave and explained that I had spoken to James and was having a lot of difficulty getting back in touch with him. Dave told me he had a conference call with James the next day, and Dave would mention that he had spoken with me and had directed me to call James; Dave would also say that he was interested in what James thought about my ideas. Now, keep in mind, I was still beating myself up mentally because I couldn't figure this out. This is why I advise you to be careful when you're doing this, because your subconscious picks up on what you're saying to yourself, and it doesn't know if you're joking or not. Either way, it will have an effect on you, I promise.

A couple days later, I got a call from Julee, Dave's wife. She was calling to apologize to me that no one had gotten back sooner with me, but they had mentioned it to James, and he was impressed with a couple of the designs. Julee had asked if anyone had let me know yet, and she was told no, they had not gotten back with me yet. Now, here's where it gets interesting. During the conference call when Dave asked James about the ideas, Dave's interest actually sparked the attention of not only the president of the company, Roger, but also of the CEO, Stephen, and both men wanted to know how far along the projects were and wanted updates. That afternoon I checked my e-mail to find a message from James requesting that I fill Roger and Stephen in on what we had discussed and that I should start communicating with Roger on all aspects of the project. So did this mean I was lucky, or did I decide to make a phone call to Dave and ask Dave to intervene on my behalf? I think you know by now where I am going with this. Luck had nothing to do with it; it was my persistence and consistency that made the difference.

Several days after that, I got another call from Julee, who wanted let me know that Stephen and James were coming into town for an event and she and Dave would be seeing them. She asked if I had any prototypes done of the apparel. I explained that no, I didn't because I had not gotten a response. So she suggested I pick out a few designs and a few styles of apparel and bring them when I was going to see her in a few weeks. She said she would be happy to show them to Stephen and James, and would give her opinion. I didn't waste another minute.

I had several design and prototyping problems to overcome, and now I had a time limit to beat. I didn't have a lot of resources, I didn't have anything drawn out yet, and the ideas were still in my head. I didn't have any way to produce one prototype, much less several items. I didn't even have one customer yet. So what did I do? You guessed it—I sat down and got deep into a good misery, and I blamed luck for not bailing me out of this. No, no, no, that is not true at all! What I really did was made a list of what I needed done and set a deadline for myself to have these things accomplished. I put a message out over social media asking for help. Yeah, can you believe that I asked for help and I didn't just wait for luck? I asked everyone I knew if they knew someone who could do embroidery or was in that business. In the meantime, I started drawing out what I thought the logo on the apparel should look like. In fact, I put together four different ideas. I then found some artwork online and began to photoshop some pictures together to create the images I wanted. In less than twenty-four hours, I had a response from my friend, saying her brother did embroidery work, had machines, and was quite good. I got his number and got in touch with him. I had seen fleece items I thought the logo designs would look good on, and as it turned out, he was able to get the items through his distribution network. I gave him the sizes and ideas that I had drawn out. Over a few days, we spoke on the phone, e-mailed, and texted each other.

The next thing I knew, I had not only one prototype, but several prototypes in different colors and sizes, and with the different ideas embroidered on the apparel. Yes, there was some cost involved, but my new embroiderer was able to get a lot of the jackets for free, as samples, and I had only had to pay for a small portion of his time when he did the embroidery. Apparently, free samples are a common practice in this business; I had no idea. It was so surreal, it was actually like seeing a dream come true. What had merely been a thought in my head was now reality. I take it back—it hadn't just been a thought, but actually an image I saw in a mirror. It was my own reflection wearing a similar jacket with another company's logo on it, but in my mind's eye, I saw this company's logo and actually had to do a double take. The second time I looked back, the logo had gone back to the original that was on the jacket. But in that moment, I saw what I needed to see. People don't understand that if you just get started, you'll see whatever you need to see too. You may not want to believe it; I didn't. But it's there and it's real; even if it seems to be only a thought, it's real. So now I had the jackets ready to go and just had to wait to take them to Chicago and drop them off with Julee for their debut appearance.

Now, while I was working on this, I went back to look at the part I really wanted to redesign. Again, I had no way to build automotive parts, and really only small connection to that industry. So I asked my embroiderer if he knew anyone who did that work. As it turns out, he did. I met with the embroiderer's contact, but it was a dead-end; however, he did give me another lead. I followed that one to a dead-end as well. Finally, I was talking to my friend at work one day when he suggested I do an online search for companies that do prototyping. So I asked to borrow his phone, and through a search engine, I came up with seven different companies who did this type of work in Michigan (where I live). Someone at the third company I called answered his phone and agreed to meet with me. I set up an appointment with him, and when the day came, I headed to see him.

When my wife and I pulled up to his building, I noticed that on his signage he had a Bible quote: "I can do all things through Christ who strengthens me" (Philippians 4:13). I have always been a believer, and this just seemed like it was too perfect to be coincidence. Who am I kidding—I heard a person say one time that "coincidence is God's way of remaining anonymous," and he was right. Anyway, my wife and I went in and met this man of large stature and his wife. I begin to explain to him what I was looking to do. When I began to tell him the story, he was immediately on board and wanted to be involved. Not only that, but he had all of his staff come into his office to hear what we were talking about doing. It was really one of the most amazing things I have ever experienced. It's funny; all I had to do was start moving in that direction, and things just began to click and work for me. Of course we hit setbacks; Murphy's Law still works and will prove its own truth to you from time to time. But it was unbelievable that this was happening, and to me!

So now that I had this company working on what could be the prototype for the project, I was off to meet up with Julee and get her opinion of the jacket ideas and designs. My dad and I headed off to Chicago. When we arrived, we took care of the other business we were there for, and then I brought out the jackets. Dave and Julee had their staff come in to look them over, and they each had their own favorite. Then Julee suggested to only go with black, to keep inventory low and costs down. I had each team member take the jacket he or she liked, including Dave and Julee, so they could be worn and so that customers could see them; I was hoping this would generate some excitement. The staff of course was very happy; who doesn't like free stuff, right? No, they were genuinely excited about the items, and to this day I still see them wearing the prototypes. It was hard to explain that none of this had been approved yet. Afterward, I left the samples with Dave and Julee, and back to Michigan I went.

After Stephen and James had seen the initial samples, Roger contacted me in order to start setting up an agreement and picking out a style. Everything was going my way until Roger discovered that I had already given samples to Dave and Julee. From this, Roger got the idea that I had already made up hundreds of these and had been selling them. I received an e-mail from him that was essentially a cease-and-desist order. I had to explain to him that James had verbally approved my pursuit of this project, and that the samples had been around, and James and Stephen both knew about them. Roger did not want to believe me. I had to call Julee and ask for more help. I explained to her what had happened. She then made a call to Stephen, who called Roger and confirmed that my story was all true. I did receive an apology e-mail from Roger, but I think you can see how a little miscommunication almost ended my idea. Either way, Roger and I were on the same page and working together again.

As it turns out, the event Dave and Julee were at wearing the prototypes was a huge success, and several people asked Julee where they could get one of those jackets. She actually told me that she could have sold probably around three hundred or more of them had they been ready to go. Did that bother me? Of course it did, but even though I had lost out on some jacket sales there, more importantly, the reaction to the jackets got the ball rolling faster. The next thing I knew, Roger was contacting

me and asking if I could send samples so that we could receive imme-
diate feedback when an idea or design was not to the sample group's
liking. This went on for about two months, and then it happened: I was
picking up my truck from the shop, and I noticed the owner's jacket with
the company logo on it. I asked to see it only to get the brand, as it was a
real eye-catcher. I got the brand, but my embroiderer could not get that
jacket through his channels. I then went and called around until finally
I went back to the shop and asked the owner where he had gotten the
jacket. He was happy to tell me, and I got in touch with the company that
made them for him, and its staff were happy to get me a couple. I had
them stitched and shipped them to Roger.

About four days later, I got an e-mail from Roger that simply said,
"Gene, you've made a winner. I guess we need to get a contract together
and get an order placed." That was almost two years ago, and I still do
work for the company, and they love the redesign I did for the compo-
nent and are going to endorse my company for it. I almost cannot believe
what happened in such a short amount of time. So should I have just sat
back and let luck take over? It seems like everything that happened, happened because of the effort that I was putting forth. I never got to just sit
around while luck swooped in and did everything for me. Please, if you
can, get the idea of luck out of your mind. It's a myth; it doesn't exist.
There was nothing lucky about what happened—I just kept trying different ways and different ideas until I found the ones that worked. When
I couldn't find any way to move forward on my own, I asked for help. I
can't even begin to imagine why anyone would put effort and time into
something and then claim he or she just got lucky. It really doesn't make
very much sense to downplay one's accomplishment in that manner. So
kick luck to the curb; it's time for it to go.

# CHAPTER 14

# EXPONENTIAL POTENTIAL

Fail means First Attempt In Learning.

AT THIS POINT I will attempt to create a separation between what you think your potential is and what your potential actually is. In all that I have seen and done, as near as I can tell, there are only really two types of potential: permanent potential and exponential potential.

So let's start with the first category, permanent potential. It really sounds great, doesn't it? I mean, to say that something is "permanent" means that it is never going to go away, right? OK, you're right to say that something permanent is by definition never going away, but that's not always a good thing. Have you ever had the experience of someone passing away and people saying, "But he or she still had so much potential." It's probably true of the person they were speaking of, but now it has become permanent potential. See, it's called "permanent potential" because there is not now, nor will there ever be, any way to recover it. The person took his or her thoughts, ideas, songs, music, movies, books, plays, inventions, and whatever else might have come into his or her mind to his or her grave. It's very unfortunate, because in the end we all suffer from the loss. We will never get to experience what that person had to offer the world, and now it's gone forever.

There are some things we do or experience—or that we don't do—that are not such good things, and I really don't think we would want them to be permanent. For example, let's say you had a permanent headache, or a permanent bill you had to pay. These are just a couple of examples, but what I am really talking about here is your potential to have and do everything and anything you want.

There are people with potential who move around this planet every day. Sometimes you can look at them and see it: these individuals will become the next big novelist, or they have already written several chart-topping songs. Some of them have planned out a new style of home nursing to help the elderly. Others still have ideas in their heads that they just haven't gotten down on paper yet—not that you really have to write all of your ideas down. However, it is a good place to start. If you at least get an idea down on paper, you can start to draw a map of where you need to go and what you need to do.

On the other hand, who says you need to get it down on paper? Just go get started, and the ways and means will come to you. I promise you, if you just take action, you'll figure it out. You can't possibly think that if you think of doing something, you don't have the skills to do it—even if you don't have all the skills necessary to do all that is required. I'm telling you, if you ask for help and look around, you will find what you need. Once you take action, you'll be surprised at what will happen for you if you just start moving toward your goal.

If you don't take the first steps and start heading toward your goals and dreams, they most likely will become permanent potential. Sometimes they don't do this, though; sometimes they will leave your head and travel to someone else's. That's right, if you don't act on these thoughts or ideas that you have, they will leave your mind, and then you'll look around one day and see your product on a store shelf, or see your invention being used by someone. You'll see this, and you'll think, *Hey that was my idea!* and it will be too late. Someone else will have gotten your idea and have run with it.

No idea, no matter how big or small it is, has come to someone in order to just die out. These things are given to you for you to accomplish. The biggest problem is that we tend to cut ourselves short in the confidence department. We begin to let fear get hold of us, and we don't have what it takes, or don't think we have what it takes, to overcome that fear. We talked about this earlier, and it's true—fear is a liar. See, the world gave you the fear you know. Think about it for a minute: We are taught to be quiet and not stand up for ourselves. We spend the majority of our lives being told what we can't do. Think back to when you were younger; from our childhood, all of us were taught all the things we couldn't do. Unfortunately, after hearing this over and over again, we begin to believe that we can't do things.

The Massachusetts Institute of Technology did a study in which the researchers found something very interesting about the human mind. Their findings break down to mean that, if a person tells you that you can't do something, sixteen additional people have to come along and tell you that you can do it. After that, the seventeenth person who comes along and tells you that you either can or can't do it is the one whom you will listen to. I would tell you to be sure that the seventeenth person is someone positive who believes in you. Hey, there's nothing that says you shouldn't move in a direction that stacks the odds in your favor!

Why not take a risk? It doesn't have to be huge; at first it could just be small, but at least you would be starting down a path toward something that may be the best thing in your life. Of course, there is an alternative to that: you may get down the path and find out you really don't like it at all. If that's the case, all you have to do is change directions. But if you don't start to try things, even things that seem insignificant, you'll never know what potential might be there for you, and if you don't start, I can guarantee it will become permanent potential.

When you stop fighting for what you want in life, everything you don't want automatically takes over, so you have to guard against the things that you talk yourself out of. You don't know where an idea will lead or what possibilities it may have for you. I was speaking with my wife the other evening, and she said to me something that was really fantastic. She had begun to stretch herself in trying something new. Now, she really fell in love with part of this new adventure and thought she would be really good at it, but it didn't turn out as planned. She said that when she got started, she discovered that there were other parts that she really had not even considered and that she was really great at, and she got more positive feedback on those parts than she did on what she thought she would be good at.

You see, had she not gotten started in what she thought she wanted to do, she would have never found the potential to still do that which she loves doing, which just ended up being a different aspect of her original idea. Had she not gotten started, it would have become permanent potential for her. That, my friends, would have been a true tragedy, mostly because of all the positive things she hears about her work and how much what she is doing is helping people who may have never gotten the help they needed otherwise. I believe she is very happy that what she began has exponential potential. This idea now has grown and expanded into areas that she had never considered instead of becoming permanent potential that has gone by the wayside—all because she got started.

I have a friend with whom, if you were to sit and speak with him, you would feel very comfortable talking to him all day long—not about anything in particular, but just about life, or hobbies, or whatever subject might come up. However, he has found himself stuck in a toxic, energy-draining relationship that he can't seem to break free from. It's one of those relationships where one person feels he or she has to dominate the other one all the time. No matter what my friend says, his wife tells him how stupid his ideas are and how much time or money he would waste in trying to accomplish them. She never gives one thought to what would make him happy, or what he could offer people if he stepped outside his comfort zone a little.

He tells me all the time that he sees the relationship is going nowhere, that it is abusive, that he doesn't think he will ever be truly happy in it. Yet he continues to stay there. You see, he's been in it all his life, and this person has beaten him down for twenty-nine years. Until now, it's all he has known. Even though he feels differently on the inside, he cannot bring himself to tell this person that it is over, that he wants to move on, that it's not good really for either of them to stay together any longer, and that honestly it hasn't been good for a while. He's afraid that he may hurt this other individual, so he stays put, keeping his mouth closed. He stays as a volunteer victim. It's very sad to see him in this situation, especially when you see all that he has to offer. You can see the excitement in his eyes when he talks about things he wants to see and do. It's a shame that if he doesn't get the courage to make the decision to move forward with his life, all of these thoughts may become permanent potential.

It's funny—in life, we are told so often about what we can't to. We are taught to be quiet and not speak up. How many times have you started to do something and had people try to talk you out of it? They say it would be too hard, or it would cost too much money, or they give some other random excuse as to why you can't do that. What I would like to help you understand here is that when people say these types of things to you, they are really speaking more about themselves rather than you. Understand that they live out of their memory the same way you do, and when they check their data banks, all they know is that at some point they were told, "No, you can't do that." So they help you by projecting their own old memories on to you as good advice.

I think people really do try to inhibit you from doing things, because they love you and don't want to see you get hurt or fail. But mostly they do this because they know you will be looking to them to help you if you fall, and they have their own agenda, which doesn't include therapy for you. But you will run across the people who love to say, "I told you so." If you do step out and try something new, and it doesn't work, they'll be the first to tell you how they knew it was a waste of time. It's funny how people who have never tried to do what you're trying to do are self-proclaimed experts on what you can or can't do. Keep in mind that if they truly had all this knowledge, they would be telling people what to do to get ahead and making money at it. But my guess is they make about as much money as you.

Why would you take the advice of someone who has only lived and seen the same things you've seen? How can such a person truly help you? I think what you'll find more often than not is that the only thing this person really wants to help you to do is stay put and be quiet, and that's no way to live. We really don't want to go through life playing it safe, tiptoeing our way to the grave. Yes, I said "grave." Because that's where we are all headed; there's no way out of it. That's the only guarantee you get: that you have to die to leave here. People are going to laugh, and gawk, and cry at you and tell you, "I told you so." I say, let them, as long as you are in pursuit of what your passion is and what will make your life meaningful to you. Then what they think about you is none of your business. You have better things to do than worry about what so-and-so might think.

If you only get started, the possibilities for what you can do and accomplish will unfold to you in ways you never dreamed of. I promise, it will almost never go the way you planned. You will have to pay Mr. Murphy of Murphy's Law his due, because he will come around to collect. But make it OK. Know going in that everything won't go as planned. Know going in that you'll have to pay your dues. Know going in that the hand at the end of your wrist is the best one you can count on. It's yours and will do as you command it to do. One time I heard a person say, "You don't have to be great to get started, but you have to get started to be great." It's true; you know in your heart of hearts that you have to get started. Whatever it is, it's calling for you. You're the one and only you who can do it, because it was given to you.

If you don't decide, and you don't get started, all of your potential becomes permanent potential. What that means is that you take it with you. When you do leave this planet, it dies with you. I bet you have heard people say, "Yeah, he or she has a lot of potential, but…" What they are really saying is that they see what that person should be, while the person remains in the area of "could be." The funny part is that we are all waiting for you to just step out. Some of us so badly need what you have to offer that we will wander around lost, waiting to see or hear what we need to in order for us to get started. Understand that we all live here on the same blue marble, and it is indeed a symbiotic circle. What effects one of us surely affects others of us.

So what effect do you want to have on people: a permanent effect or an exponential effect? Permanent potential will never affect anyone, including yourself. But what makes permanent potential worse is that because it will never have any effect, we will miss out on the wave it will send across the world to change people. What if you were the one who discovered an algorithm to solve a problem, and another person who reads your work on the subject takes that same algorithm and figures out that it can be used to understand the workings and structure of cancer better? From that, this second person shares his or her work with another person who uses the information to be able to build and accurately predict the biological structure of the processes through which and reasons why cancer forms in the human body, and from there it leads to a cure. What if something that you thought was so insignificant became something that changed the world and left an exponential effect on the entire world? Sir Isaac Newton once said, "I have seen so far because I have stood on the shoulders of giants." What he meant was that he was able to read someone else's ideas and compile them into new ways of thinking and propel us into new areas that had never been considered before. Or, of course, you can just watch another episode of some TV show and turn that exponential potential into permanent potential.

Understand that exponential potential lives on long after you and I are gone. Look back over your life; a lot of people have seen potential in you. That's why you are where you are today. There are a lot of people who have helped you because of the potential they saw in you. None of us can honestly say that no one has ever helped him or her. If anyone ever tells you that no one ever helped him or her, call that person a liar. Go ahead—I give you permission—then ask that person how he or she ever changed his or her own diaper with no knowledge of how to do so or any coordination or motor skills. Here lies the problem: if you don't do something with all the help that people have given to you, and turn that into exponential potential, then you're not just letting yourself down, you're letting others down too. They freely gave you that help so you would make a difference, not so you could spend a few more hours watching TV. Do us all a favor: don't waste your exponential potential—you're too valuable to all of us.

# CHAPTER 15

# READY

If we wait until we're ready, we'll be waiting the rest of our lives.

So YOU HAVE made it to the end, the last chapter; you now have all the information you need. Are you ready? Funny word, "ready"; I think sometimes people redefine it so that they can use it only as an excuse. You can be ready for some things, but I promise you, have never been ready for most of your life.

Let's think about this for a minute. I would like to pose a question, and please pause for a moment and reflect before answering. *When are you ever ready?* See, we can get ready to go out; you know, by doing the simple things, like shower, shave, fix our hair, put deodorant on, and so on and so on. But what I want to do is to walk back with you and take a good long look at your life, and let's see if we can count up all the things that you were or weren't ready for. How many times were you ready?

So while we take this journey, please be honest with yourself; nobody will ever know if you were or weren't honest, but *you* will, and you'll only be cheating yourself. When people decide to move on anything, this little thought comes into their mind: "Am I ready for this?" A lot of the time, this is where people stop, and the word "ready" becomes their excuse. We say things to ourselves like: "I'll be ready when I have more time." "I'll be ready when the numbers are right." "I need to have more money saved up; then I'll be ready." "When the kids are grown, I'll be ready." "I'll be ready when I graduate." "Maybe next year, things will be different; then I'll be ready." Is any of this starting to sound familiar? These may be things that you yourself have proclaimed as reasons why you're not ready.

So we began to take on this mind-set that there is some mystical starting point out there in the future. It's just waiting for us to be ready, and if we can just accomplish a few more tasks, then we'll be ready; the problem is that we never seem to get to that point where we feel comfortable enough to start. Something always seems to get in the way and mess things up. Then we have to set a new magical starting point, and the circle of doing nothing starts all over again.

Do you remember when you were a kid and you played hide-and-seek? I remember one of us would always go first, and we would have to close our eyes and count to ten; typically, then the seeker would have to go try to find everyone or else give up. Do you remember what everyone always yelled after the number ten? Without fail, they would yell, "Ready or not, here I come." Wow—ready or not, how dare they not let me get completely prepared?

Do you remember your first day of school? Were you completely prepared when Mom and Dad dropped you off at the building?

Do you remember the first time you drove a car? Well, I'm sure you were so prepared that you just jumped in and took right off.

Do you remember your first flat tire—how you were just so ready to change that flat?

Do you remember your first traffic ticket? Remember how you called to schedule that so you would be ready?

Do you remember your first car accident? I'm sure you started the week off planning for it, and then the morning of the day it was going to happen, you were completely ready. It didn't surprise you at all, did it?

Do you remember your first kiss? It went right according to plan, didn't it?

Do you remember asking for her hand in marriage? Or do you remember being asked for your hand? Just like you expected, right? Everything was so in order you couldn't help but say yes, right?

Do you remember when you found out you were going to be a mom or dad? Of course you were completely prepared for that.

Do you remember the first time you held your newborn child? Just like you planned, right?

I think we both know that I could go on and on drudging up past events that, at the end of the day, we agree we weren't ready for. So what happened: Did we fall apart? Give up? Just become stagnant? When you look at all of the events that have taken place in your life, how many can you honestly say you were ready for? If we're all being honest, my best guess is that 99 percent of the time you weren't ready. But somehow you handled it. It didn't get the best of you, whatever the circumstances or how grim the situation. You did it, and you did it while not being ready for it.

Whatever has been thrown at you in life, you handled it—not being prepared, not knowing what was coming, not having any clue of what you would do. Yet you still survived it; you made the best of whatever was given to you. You did all this with no clue of how you would do it; you just did it and took care of it.

See, when you look back over these things that have happened to you, you'll find they really weren't that difficult to handle. So the question becomes: If you can handle the things that are unexpected in your life, that just blindside you on an idle afternoon, what makes you think that you have to be ready to do something that you want to have happen to you? Something that will make you happy? Something that will give your life more meaning and value? Why do think that you need to be ready for this?

Everyone makes it. The law of averages says that if I work long enough and hard enough, I make it. There's no other way around it. You want the stats? You want the odds? It's one hundred percent of the people who decide. One hundred percent make it. All you have to do is decide; you're ready. So I ask you the question now: have you decided? Because we both know you're ready.

# THANK YOU

We're all waiting for yours.

I WANT TO take a moment to thank you, the reader. I know it seems funny that most people have forgotten about manners these days, but I want you to know that I appreciate you. I appreciate your effort in reading this. I appreciate who you are and who you're becoming. I know that you are ready for something more; you just haven't figured it all out yet, and I can't wait to see the results. Know that it's OK that you don't know it all, and march forward as if you do. We're all waiting to see what you have for us. We will all be there cheering for you—we always have been, even when you didn't see us.

# ABOUT THE AUTHOR

GENE K. J. Kopczyk overcame being labeled as a learning-disabled child to graduate from high school in 1993. While in high school, he won awards for creative writing. He earned his degree from the University of Michigan in 1999. He was asked to consider a position in the writing center at the University and also received awards for higher education while at the University of Michigan.

Gene and his wife Jennifer live in Michigan, where he now owns a multidimensional company. He and Jennifer also own For Life Health and Fitness, a fitness studio where the trainers set their own schedule and be their own boss. Kopczyk has sat on public boards in his community, and also donated time to several charitable organizations as well as the American Cancer Society and won a local Relay for Life award for the highest donations earned as a team member on the Hope Kills Cancer team.

www.ingramcontent.com/pod-product-compliance
Lightning Source LLC
LaVergne TN
LVHW091157080426
835509LV00006B/728